Arunta Art Gallery
& Book Shop
Tod... ..., Alice Springs

A FIELD GUIDE TO

CENTRAL
AUSTRALIA

A FIELD GUIDE TO

CENTRAL AUSTRALIA

Penny van Oosterzee

PHOTOGRAPHY BY

Reg Morrison

JB BOOKS **J.B. BOOKS AUSTRALIA**

A FIELD GUIDE TO
CENTRAL AUSTRALIA

This soft cover edition is an exclusive
production published in 1998
by J.B Books Pty Ltd
PO Box 118,
Marleston 5033 South Australia
Phone/Fax (08) 8297 1669
First published in soft cover in 1995
by Reed Books Australia

National Library of Australia
Cataloguing-in-Publication data

van Oosterzee, Penny
A Field Guide to Central
Australia
Includes Index
ISBN 0 7301 0479 6

1. Botany-Australia, Central.
2. Zoology-Australia, Central.
Natural history-Australia, Central.
I. Morrison, Reg
II. Title
574.9942

Edited by Mary Halbmeyer
Designed by Robert Taylor &
Linda Maclean

Typeset in Quorum Medium 8pt
by Reed Books

Printed in HK
Produced by Phoenix Offset

Contents

Introduction

Central Australia is world famous for its evocative landscape, often seen for the first time from the air. Here the subtle, swirling patterns of the vast, flat land are as mysterious as they are sublimely beautiful. On the ground, the striking natural features, magnified by the clarity of the atmosphere and thrown into stark relief by the sharpness of the sun, give the landscape its oft-spoken timeless quality.

Central Australia has its backbone in the MacDonnell Ranges, a 400-kilometre-long crumbling vertebrae of rock sunk in desert sands. To the south-east, sweeping off the Ranges in giant ribs, is the Simpson Desert. And 400 kilometres to the south-west erupts one of the great tourist icons in the world, Uluru (Ayers Rock) with its cousin Kata Tjuta (The Olgas) close by.

The wealth of plant and animal life is an unexpected surprise. Even more surprising in this ancient land, is the relative youth of its biological diversity. Most of the plants and animals of Central Australia have invaded from outside the arid zone and those that have evolved here have done so recently (geologically speaking). The result is a vigorous assemblage of plants and animals. Colourful birds—more species than found in the whole of Britain sing their presence. Lizards—Central Australia has the greatest diversity of reptiles in the world—scramble for cover. Relics of a wetter past can still be found hidden in moist oases protected from the Johnny-come-lately desert by the folds of the ancient mountains. And here, indeed, one can find the echoes of the ancient rainforest environment long since vanished.

This book provides examples of commonly seen plants and animals of Central Australia. This approach necessarily means that obvious animals such as birds will dominate the book. Apart from ants, which are the most familiar and conspicuous of all insect groups in Central Australia, other insects and arthropods have not been described.

This book is a guide, not only to what is obvious, but also to what is not so obvious. For instance, there is a section on the tracks and traces of the many nocturnal desert-dwellers. They rest during the dust-devil day, invisible in cool burrows. In what is a novel approach, *A Field Guide to Central Australia* also provides a framework, in the form of Central Australian habitats, to explain why a certain plant or animal is found where it is.

How to use this book

Central Australia's extraordinarily beautiful natural environment is the main reason people visit: about 500 000 each year. A quarter of all Australians have already visited the Centre and most of those who have never visited, wish to. Tourism is the Centre's most important industry and a potent reminder of the value of our priceless natural resources. In recognition of this, *A Field Guide to Central Australia* is based on the main tourist routes.

The book is composed of two parts. Part 1 divides the region into four subregions based on main tourist routes: west, east, south-west and south-east. These four tourist route chapters, provide base-maps on which are superimposed the five main habitats of Central Australia, which form the focus of Part 2.

The chapters of Part 1 also provide specific information, or themes, relevant to the routes of each subregion. The theme for the west subregion (West MacDonnells, Palm Valley and ring-road to Kings Canyon) is the geology, focussing mainly on rock formations. The same theme is appropriate to the east subregion (East MacDonnells). The south-west subregion (route to Uluru [Ayers Rock] and Kings Canyon from Alice Springs), on the other hand, lends itself to a theme focussing on evolution. For the south-east subregion (the route to Chambers Pillar and Andado and returning via Santa Theresa), the theme is the dunes of the northern Simpson Desert.

The raw geology of Central Australia moulds the landscape into patterns of topography, soils and vegetation. Scientifically, these patterns are referred to as 'land systems'. Most people recognise them naturally as aspects of the striking scenery. Using photography as the vehicle, the chapters of Part 1 provide a guide to the scenery in the form of land systems.

Part 2 is the main part of the book and comprises the five habitat chapters, which provide a guide to the commonly seen plants and animals of the main habitats of Central Australia:

* Desert ranges and associated foothills, including outlying hills and mesas
* Riverine woodlands
* Mulga woodlands
* Sand-dunes and sand-plains
* Chenopod shrublands and gibber plains.

The locations of these habitats are clearly detailed on the maps at the beginning of each of the tourist route chapters in Part 1, so that while driving along you can see, at a glance, which habitat you are in.

PART ONE

A GUIDE TO THE SCENERY

*The most stunning feature of Central
Australia is its scenery. Here, perhaps more
than anywhere else in the world, the scenery is a
reflection of the continent's geology. These bare
bones are variously sculpted by erosion and clothed
in different films of vegetation. Science recognises
these different patterns of geology, topography, soils
and vegetation as 'land systems'. If you travelled all
the tourist routes of Central Australia you would
pass through 34 different land systems or types of
scenery; each varying from 10 to 1000 square
kilometres. And each expresses the extent of a particular geologic formation, such as a row of sharp
ridges; or geomorphic process, such as a
flood-out of a river onto the desert plains.
From a biological point-of-view, a land system
comprises a complex of one or more ecosystems and
can therefore provide a guide to the plants and
animals that are likely to be found in it. Many of
the following photographs in Part 1 provide guides
to the scenery of Central Australia.*

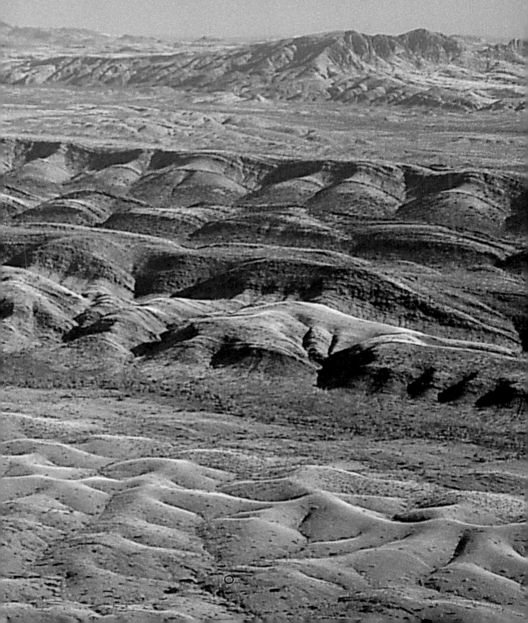

Five land systems are revealed in this Wedge-tailed Eagle's view of Central Australia. In the distant background are the massive granite and gneiss mountain ranges of the Harts Land System. In front and to the right of these is spectacular Mount Sonder after which the Sonder Land System of bold sandstone ranges has been named. The gravelly terraces of the Stokes Land System fill the valley between Mount Sonder and the striking Gillen Land System of sandstone ranges which march east–west through the centre of the picture. The spinifex-covered hills of the Pertnjara Land System fold in a crumpled apron in the foreground .

CHAPTER ONE

Alice Springs - Glen Helen - Gosse Bluff - Palm Valley - Hermannsburg - Alice Springs

A Short Geological Field Guide

About one billion years ago the ancient core of our continent was contoured into a vast basin, like a stupendous soup bowl. Into this basin up to 10 km of sediment was dumped by timeless seas and forgotten rivers. Cradling Uluru at its centre, the Amadeus Basin is vast. The road from Alice Springs to Glen Helen skirts a section of the northern edge of the Amadeus Basin.

Three hundred million years ago the Earth had a violent upheaval and 600 million years worth of flat-lying layered rock was tipped on its side during the Alice Springs Orogeny which resulted in

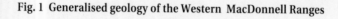

Fig. 1 Generalised geology of the Western MacDonnell Ranges

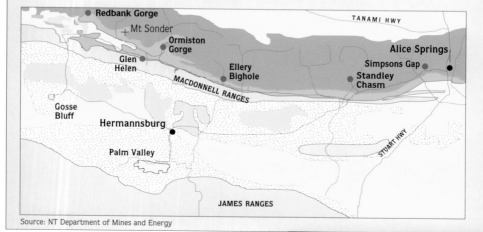

Redbank Gorge
Mt Sonder
Ormiston Gorge
Glen Helen
TANAMI HWY
Ellery Bighole
MACDONNELL RANGES
Alice Springs
Simpsons Gap
Standley Chasm
Gosse Bluff
Hermannsburg
Palm Valley
STUART HWY
JAMES RANGES

Source: NT Department of Mines and Energy

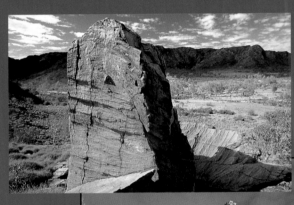

Quarternary (present to 2 m.y.o.)
development of soil and sand cover

Tertiary (65 to 2 m.y.o.)
valleys filled with freshwater lakes; silt and clay
deposited

Devonian–Carboniferous (*ca.* 350 m.y.o.)
Alice Springs Orogeny, severe mountain building; sand
and conglomerate deposited

Cambrian–Devonian (570 to 350 m.y.o.)
sandstone, siltstone, limestone deposited

Adelaidian (850 to 400 m.y.o.)
Amadeus Basin covered by sea; sand, silt, mud, lime
mud, and rare glacial sediments deposited

Lower Proterozoic (*ca.* 2000 m.y.o.)
volcanic rock deposited then igeneous rock now called
Arunta Block and includes Chewings Range Quartzite

m.y.o. = million years old

WEST SUBREGION

Mt Zeil ○

Mt Razorback ○

Redbank Gorge ○

Mt Sonder ○

Tylers Pass

Ormiston Gorge ○

Glen Helen ●

Mt Giles ○

CHEWINGS

WEST MACDONNELL

W E S T

M A C D O N N E L L

Ochre Pits ○

Serpentine ○ Gorge

Ellery Big Ho

NAMATJIRA DRIVI

R A N G E S

Gosse Bluff ○

←TO KINGS CANYON

Hermannsburg ●

KRICHAUFF

RANGE

Palm Valley ○

FINKE GORGE

NATIONAL PARK

JAMES

RANGES

Finke

River

JAM

LEVI

RANGE

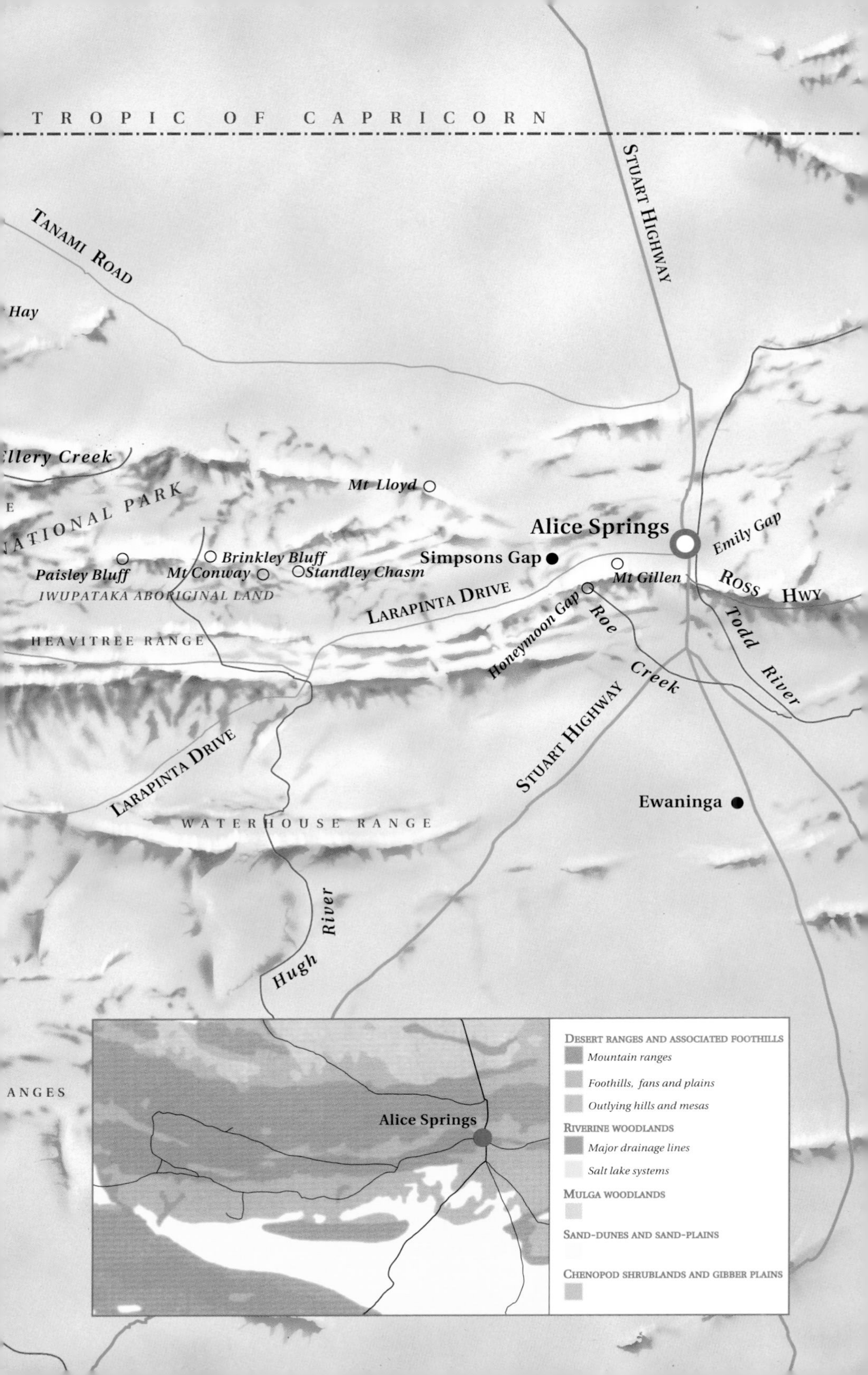

TROPIC OF CAPRICORN

STUART HIGHWAY

TANAMI ROAD

Hay

...llery Creek

...NATIONAL PARK

Mt Lloyd

Alice Springs

Emily Gap

Brinkley Bluff

Paisley Bluff   Mt Conway   Standley Chasm   **Simpsons Gap**   Mt Gillen   Ross   Hwy

IWUPATAKA ABORIGINAL LAND

LARAPINTA DRIVE

HEAVITREE RANGE

Honeymoon Gap   Roe   Creek   Todd   River

LARAPINTA DRIVE

STUART HIGHWAY

WATERHOUSE RANGE

Ewaninga

Hugh   River

...ANGES

Alice Springs

DESERT RANGES AND ASSOCIATED FOOTHILLS
- Mountain ranges
- Foothills, fans and plains
- Outlying hills and mesas

RIVERINE WOODLANDS
- Major drainage lines
- Salt lake systems

MULGA WOODLANDS

SAND-DUNES AND SAND-PLAINS

CHENOPOD SHRUBLANDS AND GIBBER PLAINS

Ellery Creek loops across the grain of the country seemingly ignoring the substantial mountain range that has risen around it.

the birth of the MacDonnell Ranges. Some of these layers are more resistant to erosion than others resulting in a landscape of edges as shown on page 13. The drive to Glen Helen is dominated by these jagged, east–west trending ridges and valleys which, surprisingly, the larger rivers cut across, running against the grain of the country.

The positions of the major watercourses were probably fixed soon after the Alice Springs Orogeny. Since then the rivers have been clawing at the rocks, stripping them down and transporting the resultant gravel, sand and silt downstream to the south and south-east. Possibly a thickness of several thousand metres of rock has been eroded from the area around Alice Springs. If, by magic, you could rebuild the mountain range with this sediment, the MacDonnell Ranges would probably be as large as the Canadian Rockies.

Below and *below right* Simpsons Gap.

While the mountains rose about them, the rivers continued to cut down across the major ridges taking advantage of any natural weaknesses.

In rivers, where water is confined when passing through resistant rocks, the erosive power of the water is much greater. Hence, deep pools are scoured in the bed immediately downstream of the gorges. Water continually permeates or seeps through the sands in the beds of the larger rivers, even though they may appear dry on top. Waterholes exist where this water seeps into a scoured-out hole.

Simpsons Gap

The brilliant-orange quartzite at Simpsons Gap is a spectacular remnant of a much more extensive, arched sheet of rock which was probably connected to the Heavitree Range which you can see 10 km to the south. The Heavitree Quartzite is the oldest layer deposited in the Amadeus Basin. Originally it was a vast, deep sheet of beach sand. It is a behemoth of a layer, extending beneath the surface, west across the Western Australian border and south to South Australia. Roe Creek eroded a gap through this quartzite at Simpsons Gap when the whole land surface was kilometres above the present level. The creek maintains its relative position as the surrounding landscape level is lowered by erosion.

Standley Chasm

Nine hundred million years ago, the Earth's crust in the region stretched.

Above and *below* Standley Chasm.

Finke Land System

The Finke Land System of sandy river plains mainly in the south of Central Australia covers around 1820 square km. Here leafy River Red Gums (*Eucalyptus camaldulensis*) grow in the sandy bed near Glen Helen Gorge.

Pertnjara Land System

The Pertnjara Land System of spinifex-covered crumpled hills in the Western MacDonnells covers around 780 square km. The hills are formed of conglomerates and are steeply rounded and around 90 m high.

Sonder Land System

The Sonder Land System of bold east–west trending sandstone ranges covers around 6000 square km through the centre of Central Australia. The ranges are formed of steeply dipping sandstone and quartzite with relief of up to 750 m. The boulder-covered slopes are dissected by parallel V-shaped valleys on which *Acacia* spp., *Senna* spp. and spinifex grow. In the valleys which are sandy to rocky, River Red Gums (*Eucalyptus camaldulensis*) and Ironwood (*Acacia estrophiolata*) grow over a variety of grasses.

Singleton Land System

The Singleton Land System is one of the most extensive land systems covering around 100 000 square km of Central Australia. It occurs mostly north of the central ranges and is a land system of gently undulating, spinifex sand-plains with a few low trees and shrubs and the occasional majestic Desert Oak *(Allocasuarina decaisneana)*. You drive through this land system from Gosse Bluff on the way round to Kings Canyon.

Vertical layers of siltstones and shales have been chemically altered to form different colours of ochre.

Serpentine Gorge winds through two layers of Heavitree Quartzite.

Magma welled up into the stretch marks. The magma cooled and formed a dark green rock called 'dolerite'. Standley Chasm was one of these stretch marks. The dolerite, being softer than the surrounding quartzite, has long been eroded away, leaving the sheer walls that vibrate with colour in the midday sun. No dolerite can be seen in the chasm. You can, however, see a slab of dolerite squeezed into the surrounding rock on the side of the road approximately 2.2 km from the kiosk at the top of the hill, just past the large creek crossing.

Ellery Big Hole

Ellery Creek, flowing southwards across the rock formations, has cut a gap in the Heavitree Quartzite ridge. The ridge is slightly offset across the waterhole, showing that a fault 'broke' the formation, making it weaker than the rocks on either side. The creek, which was flowing across a higher land surface long ago, has taken advantage of this and has cut down at the weakest point along the ridge.

Several spectacular examples of the Earth's force, where rock has been squeezed like geological toothpaste, can be seen here. In the gap itself the Heavitree Quartzite is almost folded back onto itself. And looking west from the car park across Ellery Creek, several folds of softer limestone can be seen. This grey rock is known as Bitter Springs Limestone.

Just before you pull back onto the highway after visiting Ellery Big Hole, have a look across the main road. You'll be able to see a wall of limestone with holes in it. With a healthy imagination, a figure of a lizard can be made out. Geologists call this lizard 'Julie'. This is because the shape is formed in what is known as the Julie Formation of limestone and siltstone. The siltstone has been eroded away leaving the shape.

You'll notice that the road generally follows a valley. This was formed where most of the underlying rocks are shales which are easily weathered and hence are 'valley-forming'.

20

BRUCE THOMSON

Serpentine Gorge

Two gorges occur here where a south-flowing creek cuts through two ridges of Heavitree Quartzite. At the upstream site, the very narrow gap indicates that the creek has eroded along a nearly straight, vertical joint.

Ochre Pits

Like all the rocks in this region, the silt-stones and shale beds have been tipped

The quartzite walls of narrow Red Bank Gorge glow in the midday sun.

up vertically. Weathering of the siltstone and shale has caused the rock to change chemically. In particular, iron oxides (common rust) were moved and affected by water-related processes. The various colours are caused by different iron oxides combining with water and staining the mineral particles in the rock.

Ormiston Gorge

The geology here is very complex. Essentially, gargantuan earth movements have heaved and thrust hundreds of metres of Heavitree Quartzite on top of itself. At the main waterhole, the Heavitree Quartzite in the base of the cliffs is overlain by more Heavitree Quartzite which has been thrust or pushed southwards from several kilometres away. The surface where the two layers sit on top of each other is at the change in slope about half-way up the main rock face.

The same complex geology has formed the spectacularly beautiful Mount Sonder and Red Bank Gorge which slashes Mount Sonder's western flank.

The shimmering white trunk of a Ghost Gum contrasts with the brick red of the massive Heavitree Quartzite of Ormiston Gorge.

Gillen Land System

The Gillen Land System of sandstone ranges and valleys trending east–west through the centre of Central Australia covers around 9700 square km. The ridges are formed of hard rocks such as quartzite and sandstone, up to 300 m high, and the valleys are eroded into the softer shales and siltstones. The ridges are covered by sparse shrubs and low trees—mainly *Acacia* spp. over spinifex and grasses and herbs. In the valleys, *Eucalyptus* spp. and *Acacia* spp. grow over grasses and spinifex.

The Finke River at Glen Helen Gorge cuts through 500-million-year-old Pacoota Sandstone.

Glen Helen Gorge

Here the Finke River has eroded a gorge across layers of Pacoota Sandstone which originally accumulated as sand at the bottom of a 500-million-year-old sea. A deep hole has been scoured by the heightened erosive forces of the river as it squeezes through the narrow gap. Water which constantly percolates through the sand of the Finke keeps the waterhole full.

Gosse Bluff

This feature is one of Central Australia's best-kept secrets. It is one of the most significant and best comet-impact structures in the world. A good view of the structure can be seen from the Tylers Pass trig station, 16 km north of the Bluff. Gosse Bluff is an erosional remnant of a large crater produced by the impact of a frozen ball of carbon dioxide, ice and dust which smacked into the Earth around 130 million years ago, releasing the energy equivalent of one million times more powerful than the Hiroshima bomb. Rock from more than 6 km down was blasted to the surface at the impact site which became the core

Known as Tnorala by its Traditional Owners, Gosse Bluff (below and right) is a magnificent remnant of a comet collision 130 million years ago.

Fig. 2. Geological map and cross-section of Gosse Bluff

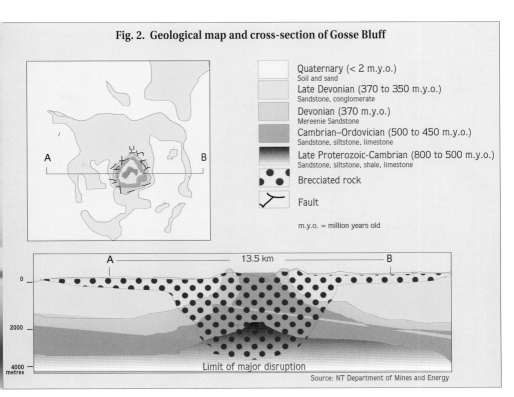

Quaternary (< 2 m.y.o.)
Soil and sand

Late Devonian (370 to 350 m.y.o.)
Sandstone, conglomerate

Devonian (370 m.y.o.)
Mereenie Sandstone

Cambrian–Ordovician (500 to 450 m.y.o.)
Sandstone, siltstone, limestone

Late Proterozoic-Cambrian (800 to 500 m.y.o.)
Sandstone, siltstone, shale, limestone

Brecciated rock

Fault

m.y.o. = million years old

Source: NT Department of Mines and Energy

of a large crater. The more resistant of this core rock, forming a ring of hills, is what you see today. The outer rim has long since been erased by erosion, though satellite imagery reveals a large halo which probably represents the

Melaleuca trichostachya (*above*) and *Pimelia interioris* (*below*) are rare plants found in Palm Valley.

BRUCE THOMSON

The springs of Palm Valley seep from sandstone aquifers and create an oasis for around 350 species of plant and a crop of 3000 Red Cabbage Palms.

extent of affected rock, indicating that the original crater was some 20 km across.

From Gosse Bluff the road continues more or less south-east to meet the road to Hermannsburg where you also have the option of heading west toward the ring-road to Kings Canyon.

Palm Valley

South of Hermannsburg, the Hermannsburg Sandstone has been folded into a range of hills. The Finke River and its tributaries have eroded a gorge through the hills. Before the hills were formed, the Finke snaked south in wide meanders. The meanders of the ancient river have been preserved in the shapes of these gorges because uplift of the hills was very slow and the rivers

BRUCE THOMSON

Palm Valley springs and Red Cabbage Palms.

Psilotum nudum (inset) and *Doodia caudata* are both rare plants.

continued downwards at the same rate as uplift occurred. In Palm Valley itself, prominent vertical rock faces were made when undercutting of the base of the hills was followed by collapsing of rock from above, back to the vertical joints.

The layers of rock in this region store water like a sponge. These aquifers seep water, like blood from a gash, where a river valley, gorge or creek cuts into them. Such sheltered habitats are known as 'refuges' because they provide havens or refuges for a variety of plants from the harsh surrounding conditions.

Palm Valley is a particularly important refugium. It provides refuge for a crop of around 3000 Red Cabbage Palms *(Livistona mariae)* found nowhere else in the world. The nearest relative is found 1000 km away. A quarter of all the plant species recorded from Central Australia have been collected from Palm Valley. Twenty-two of these are classified as rare and thirteen as relict.

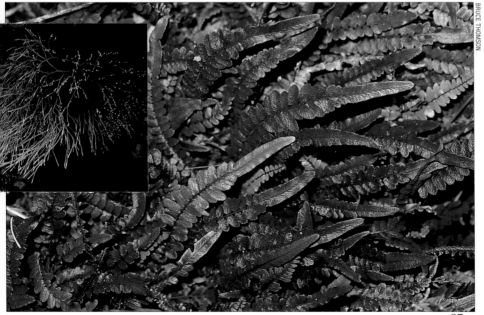

BRUCE THOMSON

CHAPTER TWO

Alice Springs - Arltunga - 'The Garden' - Stuart Highway - Alice Springs

A Short Geological Field Guide

East of Alice Springs, the Ross Highway follows the low ground along the southern flank of the MacDonnell Ranges. To the left, the steep, flat rock faces on the range were once horizontal layers of essentially beach sand of a shallow sea which existed about 850 million years ago. This beach sand was virtually pressure-cooked into the conspicuous, orange-coloured Heavitree Range.

Bitter Springs Formation

Between the road and red quartzite ridges are grey outcrops of limestone of what is known as the Bitter Springs Formation. Countless years of rain have dissolved this rock to produce the deep grooves seen down the sides of the outcrop.

Corroboree Rock.

Corroboree Rock

Corroboree Rock is a pillar of limestone which has been more resistant to erosion than the surrounding shale.

Trephina Gorge Nature Park

The upstanding nature of Heavitree Quartzite is clearly seen in Trephina Gorge Nature Park. Of great interest is the fact that the normal sequence of younger rocks over older rocks has been

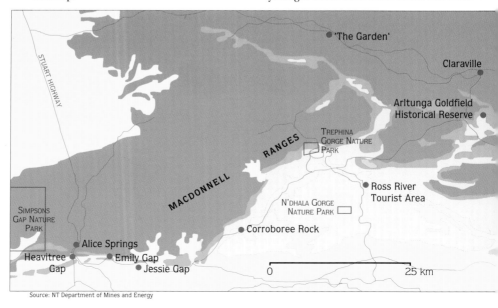

Source: NT Department of Mines and Energy

The Arltunga Historical Reserve

The turn-off to Arltunga leads first through strongly folded, grey, limestone rocks of the Bitter Springs Formation. Different layers in this formation have differing hardnesses. The hardest, most resistant layers form ridges and the softer ones form furrows. These ridges and furrows are obvious on the hillsides where they form a curved pattern. Limestone has given rise to jagged skylines while sandstone and siltstone have produced more rounded profiles.

In places the grey limestone of the Bitter Springs Formation forms columns of fossil stromatolites. Living forms of these mounds of cyanobacteria still exist in Shark Bay, Western Australia.

disturbed so that, in the hills to the north of the Gorge, ancient granite deposited one billion years before the Bitter Springs Limestone, lies on top of it; a reminder of the extraordinary strength of earthly convulsions.

Ross River Geology

At Ross River Homestead, a gorge has been cut through a series of sedimentary rocks, in which all beds or layers slope southwards. These were deposited between 500 and 350 million years ago as mud, sand and lime in a shallow sea.

At Emily Gap the Heavitree Quartzite provides a spectacular canvas for Aboriginal art.

Fig. 3. Geology and Landforms of the East MacDonnell Ranges

Sand, soil, laterite, alluvium

Bedded sediments

Upstanding heavitree quartzite

Uneven metamorphic rocks

EAST SUBREGION

SANDOVER HIGHWAY

STUART HIGHWAY

PLENTY HIGHWAY

STRANGWAYS RANGE

BURT   PLAIN

TROPIC OF CAPRICORN

TANAMI ROAD

Mt Benste

SIMPSONS GAP
NATIONAL PARK

Mt Lloyd ○

Corroboree Rock ○

Alice Springs ◉

CORROB
ROCK
CONSERVA
RESERVE

Simpsons Gap ●

Emily Gap

Mt Undoolya ○

Brinkley Bluff ○

Mt Gillen ○

EMILY & JESSIE GAPS
NATURE PARK

Mt Conway ○

Standley
Chasm ○

Honeymoon
Gap ○

Ross   HIGHWAY

NAMATJIRA DRIVE

LARAPINTA DRIVE

○ Mt Ertwa

OORAMINN
RANGE

LARAPINTA DRIVE

River

Ewaninga ●

PHILLIPSO
POUND

Hugh

EWANINGA
ROCK CARVINGS
CONSERVATION
RESERVE

WATERHOUSE
RANGE

STUART HIGHWAY

**Santa
Teresa** ●

DESERT RANGES AND ASSOCIATED FOOTHILLS

Mountain ranges

Foothills, fans and plains

Outlying hills and mesas

RIVERINE WOODLANDS

Major drainage lines

Salt lake systems

MULGA WOODLANDS

SAND-DUNES AND SAND-PLAINS

CHENOPOD SHRUBLANDS AND GIBBER PLAINS

Alice Springs

HARTS RANGE

'The Garden'

HALE PLAIN

GINA RANGE

'Claraville'

Ambalindum

ARLTUNGA HISTORICAL RESERVE

Arltunga Gold Mines

MORDOR POUND

PADDIES PLAIN

ATNARPA RANGE

RUBY GORGE NATURE PARK

TREPHINA GORGE NATURE PARK

Ross River Homestead

N'DHALA GORGE NATURE PARK

EAST MACDONNELL RANGES

Todd River

Huckitta Land System

The Huckitta Land System of rugged limestone ranges in the east-central part of Central Australia covers around 1600 square km. Its steeply dipping and often contorted limestone hills reach a height of up to 225 m. Sparse shrubs and trees such as this Ghost Gum grow over prickly spinifex.

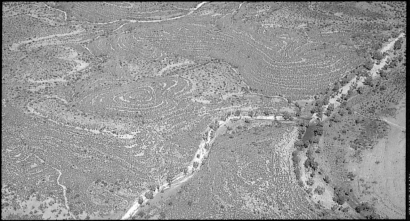

GRANT ALLAN

Allua Land System

The Allua Land System is similar to the Huckitta Land System but has a lower relief of up to 90 m and the ridges and hills are more disorganised. From the air, this land system reveals striking patterns etched by vegetation.

Boen Land System

The gently undulating mulga-covered plains that you traverse along the Stuart Highway north of Alice Springs are part of the Boen Land System of red earth plains. The Mulga (*Acacia aneura*) which mantles these plains forms groves that, from the air, form a pattern like a giant's fingerprint.

Todd Land System

[T]odd Land System of timbered plains and flood-outs of the Todd River, here [runni]ng through The Gap of Alice Springs, covers an area of around 780 square [km. Land] systems can be broken down into units and this land system can be [brok]en down into eight units from the extensive outer flood plains which have [tree]s and bushes such as *Acacia* spp. over grasses, to the main channel in which [River] Red Gum *(Eucalyptus camaldulensis)* and Coolibah *(Eucalyptus coolibah [subsp.] arida)* grow. In between are a variety of units including dunes, distributary

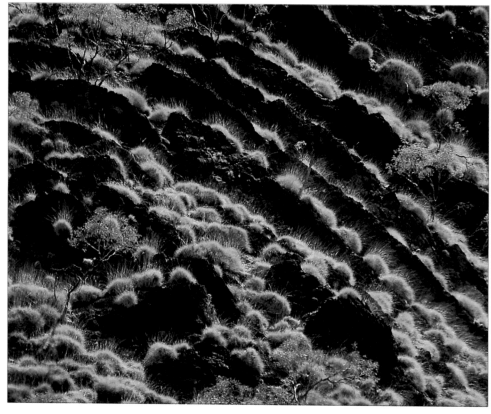

Along this road you can also see the original ancient granitic rocks which are about 1.8 billion years old. Their history has been one of stress and deep burial, resulting in some of the original minerals altering. Mica, which is a flattish, black, shiny mineral has developed widely here and gives the rocks their flaky or slab-like texture.

Spinifex growth defines anticlinal fold, East MacDonnell Ranges.

The road climbs out of the river valley, up a low rise and onto a completely flat plain of grass called Paddy's Plain, which is surrounded by large hills. The white hills to the east are called White Range and are made of resistant white quartzite.

The Arltunga Historical Reserve, is an old gold mining area and the granite in the region has weathered to a gentle, hummocky surface. This is shot through with conspicuous white quartz reefs where the gold was found.

The road continues north to Claraville across crystalline granite. The upstanding white quartz reefs are very noticeable along this section of the road.

At Claraville, the road branches to the west and crosses the flat Hale River Plain. The route progresses over the granite toward the Stuart Highway and Alice Springs. To the north you can see the Strangways Range, also composed of ancient granite.

Alice Springs - Uluru - Kings Canyon

A Guide to Evolution

The Stuart Highway

The route from Alice Springs to Uluru is a journey through time. You drive through one of the most ancient landscapes on Earth, passing time-worn stubs of once Canadian Rocky-sized mountains. In places you can step out of your vehicle and see fossils of the earliest life forms on the planet.

The rounded, boulder-strewn hills around Alice Springs, particularly to its north are composed of Alice Springs Granite, a granular rock of mottled white, grey, pink and black grains or crystals. At around 1800 million years old, these rocks are some of the oldest on the planet. They were originally formed from molten rock which slowly cooled 10 to 15 km below the surface of the earth.

Much later, after two mountain ranges had come and gone, Central Australia sank beneath a vast sea. A blanket of coarse sand, 800 m thick, made up in part from the residues of these ancient mountains, was deposited on top of their worn-down roots. The sand was later buried and heated—virtually pressure-cooked—before being exposed once again as a quartzite. Heavitree Quartzite forms the orange cliffs shadowing Alice Springs to the south. The Gap through which all traffic from the south must pass to reach Alice Springs is called the Heavitree Gap.

Two kilometres south of the Gap is Mount Blatherskite, on the east of the

The rounded, boulder-strewn hills in the foreground, are around 1800 million years old. The Heavitree Range showing 'The Gap' of Alice Springs is in the background.

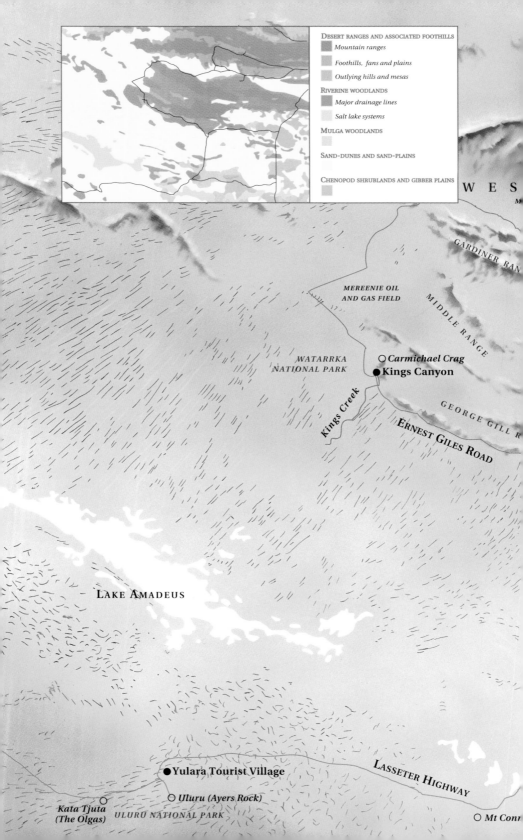

DESERT RANGES AND ASSOCIATED FOOTHILLS

Mountain ranges

Foothills, fans and plains

Outlying hills and mesas

RIVERINE WOODLANDS

Major drainage lines

Salt lake systems

MULGA WOODLANDS

SAND-DUNES AND SAND-PLAINS

CHENOPOD SHRUBLANDS AND GIBBER PLAINS

W E S

GARDINER RAN

MIDDLE RANGE

MEREENIE OIL
AND GAS FIELD

WATARRKA
NATIONAL PARK

○ Carmichael Crag
● Kings Canyon

GEORGE GILL R

Kings Creek

ERNEST GILES ROAD

LAKE AMADEUS

● Yulara Tourist Village

LASSETER HIGHWAY

Kata Tjuta
(The Olgas)

○ Uluru (Ayers Rock)

ULURU NATIONAL PARK

○ Mt Conr

SOUTH-WEST SUBREGION

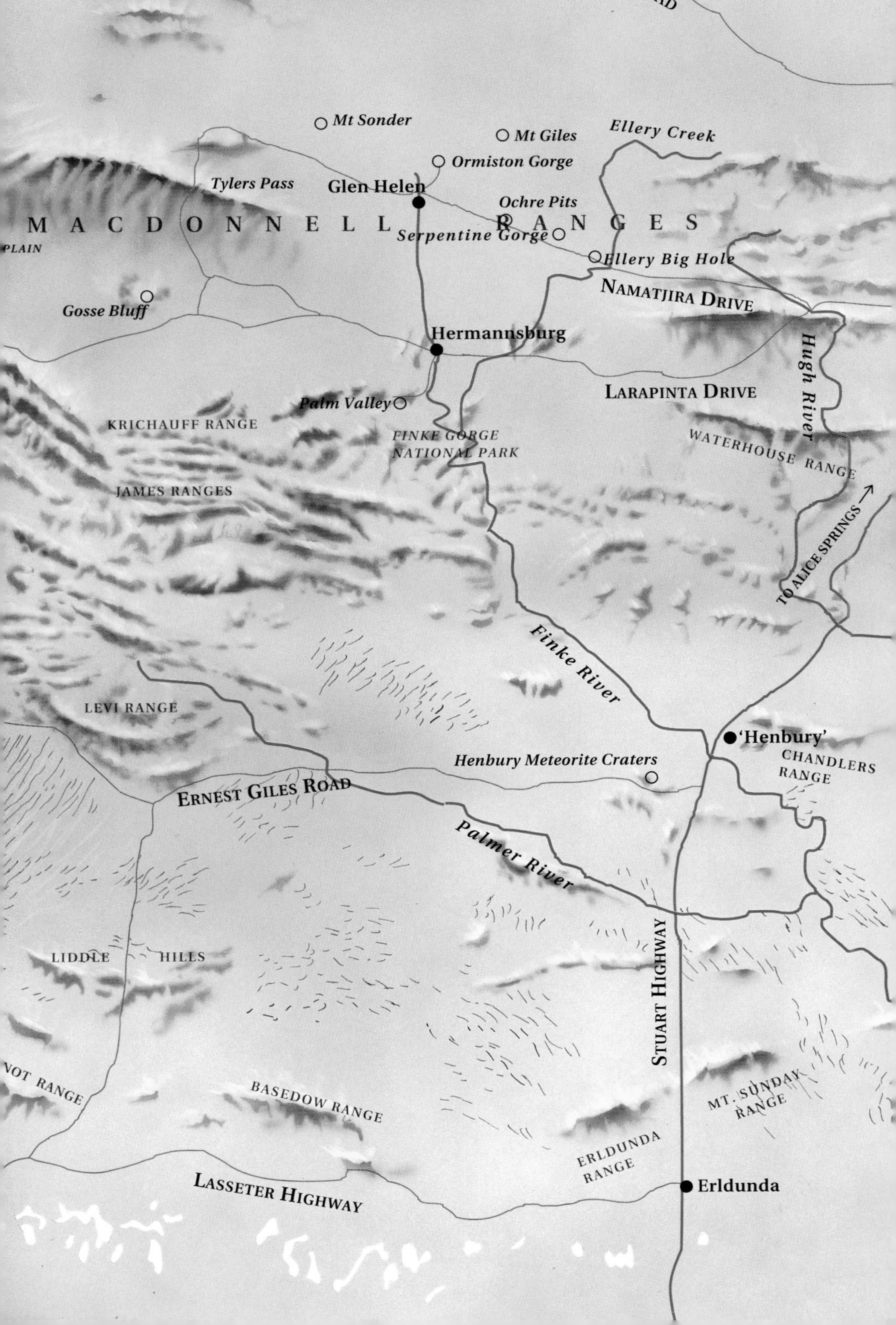
Tanami Road
Mt Sonder
Mt Giles
Ellery Creek
Ormiston Gorge
Tylers Pass
Glen Helen
Ochre Pits
MACDONNELL RANGES
PLAIN
Serpentine Gorge
Ellery Big Hole
Namatjira Drive
Gosse Bluff
Hermannsburg
Hugh River
Larapinta Drive
Palm Valley
KRICHAUFF RANGE
FINKE GORGE NATIONAL PARK
WATERHOUSE RANGE
JAMES RANGES
TO ALICE SPRINGS
Finke River
LEVI RANGE
'Henbury'
Henbury Meteorite Craters
CHANDLERS RANGE
Ernest Giles Road
Palmer River
LIDDLE HILLS
Stuart Highway
NOT RANGE
BASEDOW RANGE
MT. SUNDAY RANGE
ERLDUNDA RANGE
Erldunda
Lasseter Highway

road. This hill was formed during the
MacDonnell Ranges Orogeny. Three
hundred million years ago, when only
amphibians and reptiles ruled the land,
violent contortions of the Earth's crust
threw up the MacDonnell Ranges. The
horizontal beds of rock were tipped vertically on their sides. Mount Blatherskite
is an excellent example of the contorted
birth of a mountain range.

The course of the major rivers,
including the Todd River, were probably
fixed in a north–south direction soon
after the MacDonnells were formed.
Today's east–west ridges were deeply
buried within the Canadian Rocky-sized
mountains. After millions of years, erosion stripped away the overlying rocks,
exposing them. The rivers, flowing perpendicular to the line of mountains,
have managed to maintain their flow
against the grain of the land by exploit-
ing any cracks in the ridges and opening
them into the spectacular gaps that you
see today.

When the MacDonnells were
formed they pushed and buckled the
rocks to the south into folds, geologically known as anticlines. Over time, the
tops of these anticlines have been
planed off by erosion, leaving the roots
jutting out as indicated in Figure 4.

There are several places along the
route where you can find 435- to 600-
million-year-old fossil invertebrates,
notably where the highway cuts a
swathe through the James Ranges and in
a gutter on the east side of the road just
north of Maloney Creek. During the life-
time of these now fossilised animals, a
shallow seaway known as the
Larapintine Sea, extended right across
Central Australia—which straddled the

480-million-year-old
fossil gastropod
(Raphistoma brownii).

520-million-year-old fossil
trilobite head (Xystridura sp.)

Fossils of the Larapintine Sea

480-million-year-old fossil nautiloid (*Madiganella tatei*)

Fossil worm trails.

520-million-year-old fossil trilobite (*Xystridura* sp.).

Fig. 4.
Formation of parallel ranges such as the MacDonnell Ranges

Anticlinal Fold

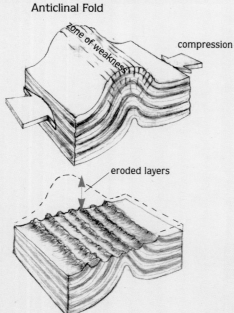

form the western extremity of the Simpson Desert. The sand is essentially all that remains of the huge mountain ranges that once straddled the continent. For millions of years it has been carried down and dumped in low-lying areas by huge rivers only to be blown back over the landscape during the last Ice Age. Since then the dunes have been stabilised by vegetation and are now immobile.

Surprisingly, these dominant land forms of Australia's arid zone are quite young. The dunes of the Simpson Desert, for instance, are only about 25 000 years old.

Fig. 5.
Formation of Kata Tjuta and Uluru

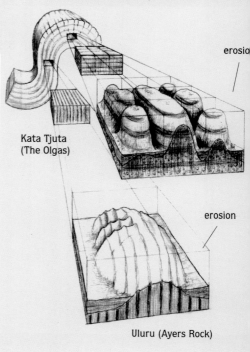

equator at the time. This tropical sea was seething with life. Indeed, on a hill nearby the Finke River is found the oldest vertebrate in the world. The sands were riddled with worms and the mud of the sea bottom became a grave for the lamp shells, molluscs, nautiloids, trilobites and many other animals that you can pick up along the route.

Upper sections of the Finke River itself are about 350 million years old, making it one of the oldest rivers in the world. If you were around at the time you might have seen the first of the land colonists step out from the sea.

The sand-dunes in this region trend generally north–south in the direction of the prevailing winds. These dunes

The Lasseter Highway

From Erldunda to Uluru (Ayers Rock), you are travelling through an immense valley floor. Over at least 100 million years the valley has been filled with gravels (which form today's gibber plains), loams and sand respectively eroded from the once giant MacDonnell Ranges.

Rainbow Valley in the James Ranges is in the Gillen Land System of parallel east–west trending ridges. Note that the sands of the Simpson Desert have blown over the ridges, an event which probably took place around 20 000 years ago during the last Ice Age.

The major topographical feature on this highway is the Lake Amadeus fossil lake system. About 14 million years ago

The native cat, or marsupial quoll (Dasyurus geoffroii) is now extinct in Central Australia. It was a close relative of this Spotted-tailed Quoll (Dasyurus maculatus) of eastern Australia whose numbers are also declining. If you had done this trip from Alice Springs to Uluru 100 years ago you might have seen up to 12 native medium-sized mammals, like the quoll, bandicoots, bettongs, wallabies and even the common brush-tailed possums. Some of these vanished as recently as 30 years ago.

Finke Land System

The Finke Land System extends in a sinuous line for hundreds of kilometres through Central Australia. The seven units which make up this land system include active inner plains on which chenopods grow; outer plains and levees on which Ghost Gums *(Eucalyptus papuana)* grow; alluvial basins and distributary channels in which Coolibahs *(Eucalyptus coolibah* ssp. *arida)* grow; and the main channel in which River Red Gums *(Eucalyptus camaldulensis)* grow.

Krichauff Land System

GRANT ALLAN

The Krichauff Land System of strongly dissected sandstone plateaux can be seen along the Ernest Giles Road and contains many of the hidden springs and oases which make this area one of the most important refuges in all of Central Australia. The Krichauff Land System covers around 8000 square km in the central ranges and while low, at up to 150 m, is one of the most rugged of land systems.

The Amadeus Land System of salt pans and fringing dunes covers around 4700 square km. The pan floors are bare, water-logged, saline clays. Melaleuca, samphire and chenopods grow on the lake margins and shrubs including *Senna* spp. and *Acacia* spp. and trees including Melaleuca and Desert Oak grow over spinifex on the fringing dunes.

"We could see the lake stretching away east-south-east as far as the glasses could carry the vision. Here we made another attempt to cross, but the horses were all floundering about in the bottomless bed of this infernal lake before we could look round. I felt sure they would be swallowed up before our eyes. We were powerless to help them for we could not get near owing to the bog, and we sank up over our knees, where the crust was broken, in hot salty mud."

Ernest Giles, Lake Amadeus, 1872.

Chandlers Land System

The flat-topped hills and stony lowlands of the Chandlers Land System occupy around 2600 square km in the south of Central Australia. You can see it along the Stuart Highway at the Chandlers Range. The flat-topped hills in this land system are capped by a tough duricrust. On the rocky slopes *Eremophila* spp. and *Hakea* spp. grow over prickly chenopods such as *Sclerolaena* spp.

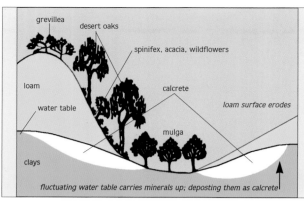

grevillea
desert oaks
spinifex, acacia, wildflowers
loam
calcrete
loam surface erodes
water table
mulga
clays

fluctuating water table carries minerals up; deposting them as calcrete

**Fig. 6.
Desert Vegetation**

The loams have mulga woodlands growing on them. Where calcrete exerts a dominant influence, Desert Oak and different *Acacias* (*Ptilotus* sp.) grow as well as pussy-tails and grasses. Sand-dunes have spinifex and shrubs growing on them.

it was a vast freshwater lake system pouring into a tropical Finke River. Today the lakes are much withered, salt lakes which, nevertheless, form a topographic feature on a continental scale; from a satellite it resolves into a linear feature 500 km long with a total area of evaporative salt lake surface of 1750 square km. The Lake Amadeus salt lake system has a catchment area of almost 100 000 square kilometres.

The cement-like calcrete benches appearing high and dry in the sand-dunes along the Lasseter Highway indicate old groundwater levels. Right across the arid zone, benches like these etch the path of ancient valleys. Many of these from a time when Amazonian-like rivers carved their way across the now vast sand-plains. The calcrete also influences which plants grow (see Figure 6).

About 150 km along the Lasseter Highway you come across a startling table-top mountain. This is Mount Conner which is often mistaken for Uluru by eager first-time visitors. Mount Conner is made of nearly flat-lying beds of sandstone, originally dumped by the meltwater of a glacier around 750 million years ago; much of Australia lay under ice near the north pole at this time. Mount Conner is called a mesa, however, it is in reality bowl-shaped and slides away to the south in a series of gullies. From the top of of Uluru (Ayers Rock) you can see

that Kata Tjuta (The Olgas) and Mount Conner are in a straight line. Because of this, most people assume some sort of connection. There is, in fact, no connection at all. Mount Conner is some 150 million years older than Uluru and Kata Tjuta and formed when Australia lay near the North Pole. Uluru and Kata Tjuta were deposited by the debris torn off mountains to the south by torrential rivers when Australia had rafted back toward the equator.

Watarrka National Park

Watarrka (Kings Canyon) National Park encompasses the western edge of the rugged George Gill Range, which includes the scenically splendid Kings Canyon with its attractive waterholes and areas of lush vegetation. Watarrka is the Luritja Aboriginal name for the Umbrella Bush, *Acacia ligulata* and the area in the vicinity of Kings Canyon.

The 100 metre towering walls of Kings Canyon have been sliced through

Spectacular beehive-like rock formations occur on top of Kings Canyon.

Kings Canyon can be reached from the Lasseter Highway or the Stuart Highway via Ernest Giles road.

two ancient sandstones. The predominant rock of the region is 360-million-year-old Mereenie Sandstone. This whitish sandstone sits on top of a lower, more rubbly red to light brown sandstone called Carmichael Sandstone which was deposited 440 million years ago. Both sandstones are clearly visible in the Canyon cliff face.

They were deposited by a vast, shallow inland sea and the Carmichael Sandstone features the fossilised tracks of ancient creatures called Trilobites similar in appearance to the Moreton Bay Bug. In the Mereenie Sandstone the very movement of the sea has been trapped in rock in the form of obvious ripple marks. At the top of the range, spectacular examples of cross bedding and the odd wander-path of an ancient worm also confirm that the rock had its birth as grains of sand beneath a shallow sea.

The sandstone domes at the top of the range have formed in areas where

View from the north face of Mount Conner.

cracks or joints in the rock form a criss-cross pattern, thus allowing quicker erosion into block shapes. Wind and rain have then eroded the corners and sides of the blocks to form domes.

Mereenie Sandstone is porous—if you could wring it, it would drip—and has stored quantities of fresh water. This is released slowly to produce the permanent springs and rockholes associated with the George Gill Range. This, and the fact that the park contains overlapping floristic regions of the western deserts, MacDonnell Ranges and Simpson Desert results in an exceptional diversity of plant communities: over 600 species of plant occur of which over 60 are rare or relict.

This is by far the richest area for plant diversity in the whole of the arid zone of Australia. Both bird and reptile communities contain scientifically important overlaps between the faunas of the western deserts and the central ranges. Over 100 species of bird flit amongst the woodlands of gorges, valleys and sand-plains, and around 60 species of reptile dart amongst the spinifex and low shrubs of the rocky plateaux and valleys. Of the larger animals, rock-wallabies and Euros, can be seen with sightings of Red Kangaroo common on the plains during good seasons.

45

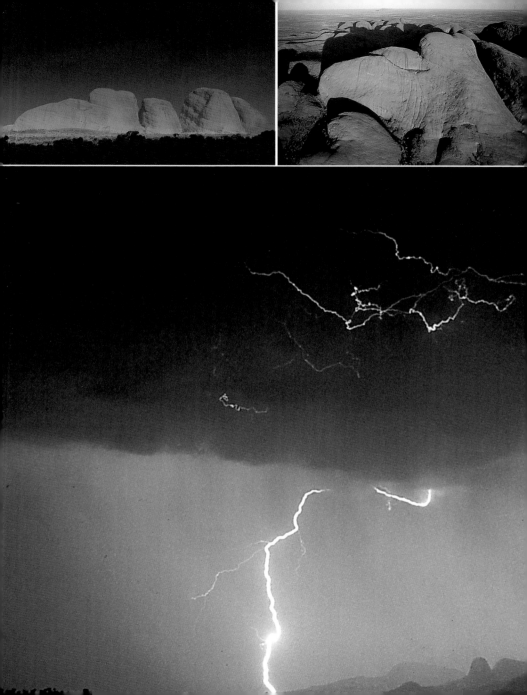

Uluru (Ayers Rock) and Kata Tjuta (The Olgas) were
formed by the debris torn off Himalayan-sized
mountains to the south by torrential storms when
Australia lay near the equator 600 million years ago.

Born in a torrential environment, the more gentle caress
of today's storms still mould the shape of the world's
most famous monolith.

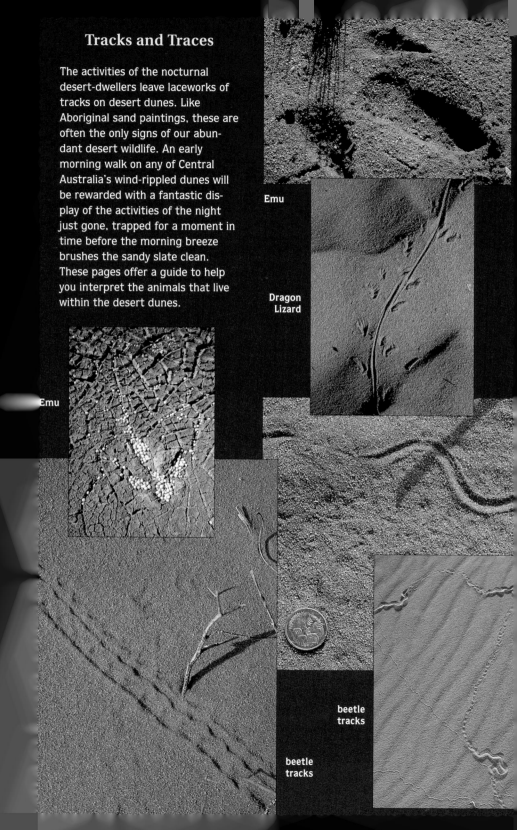

Tracks and Traces

The activities of the nocturnal desert-dwellers leave laceworks of tracks on desert dunes. Like Aboriginal sand paintings, these are often the only signs of our abundant desert wildlife. An early morning walk on any of Central Australia's wind-rippled dunes will be rewarded with a fantastic display of the activities of the night just gone, trapped for a moment in time before the morning breeze brushes the sandy slate clean. These pages offer a guide to help you interpret the animals that live within the desert dunes.

Emu

Dragon Lizard

Emu

beetle tracks

beetle tracks

cockroach tracks

beetle track markers

small mammal

Legless Lizard

Mole Cricket

beetle tracks

beetle tracks

Tracks and Traces

Dingo

beetle tracks

beetle tracks and Rabbit tracks

Spinifex Hopping Mouse

Native Mouse

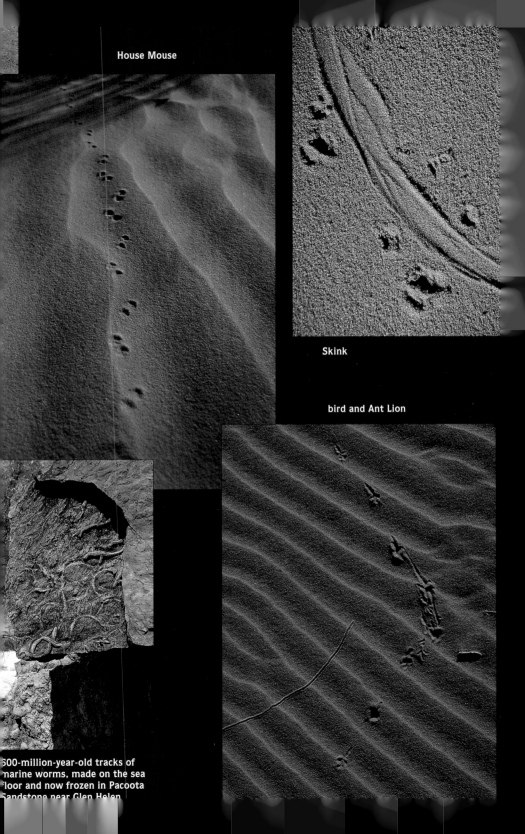

House Mouse

Skink

bird and Ant Lion

500-million-year-old tracks of marine worms, made on the sea floor and now frozen in Pacoota Sandstone near Glen Helen

CHAPTER FOUR

Alice Springs - Andado - Alice Springs

A Guide to the Dunes

The trip from Alice Springs along the Old Ghan Line to Chambers Pillar, New Crown and Andado is a trip into the largest sand-ridge desert in the world: the Simpson Desert. This is the driest region of Central Australia. The dune fields of the Simpson Desert cover an area of 159 000 square km. The dunes are straight, parallel and evenly spaced, trending 334 to 340 degrees and running continuously for up to 200 km. Spacing ranges from 200 m to over 1 km with dunes on this route through the northern section of the Desert being about 300 to 400 m apart. Dune junctions open downwind.

Sand-dunes.

Simpson Desert.

GRANT ALLAN

54

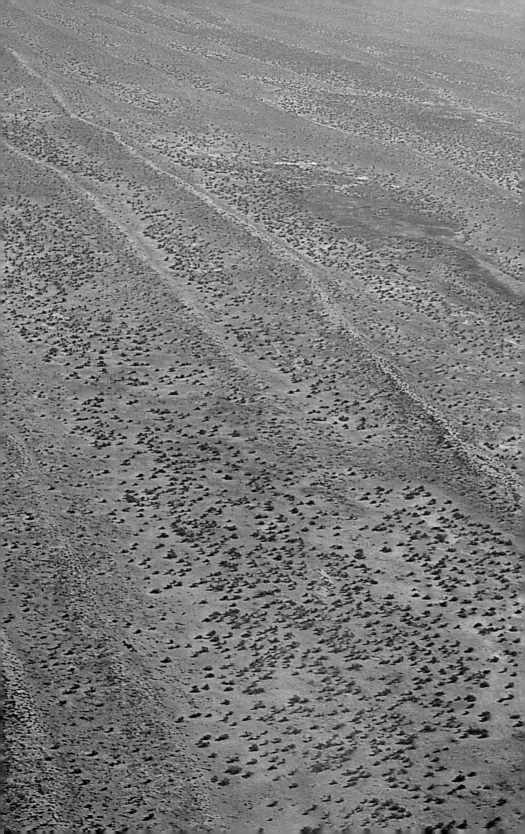

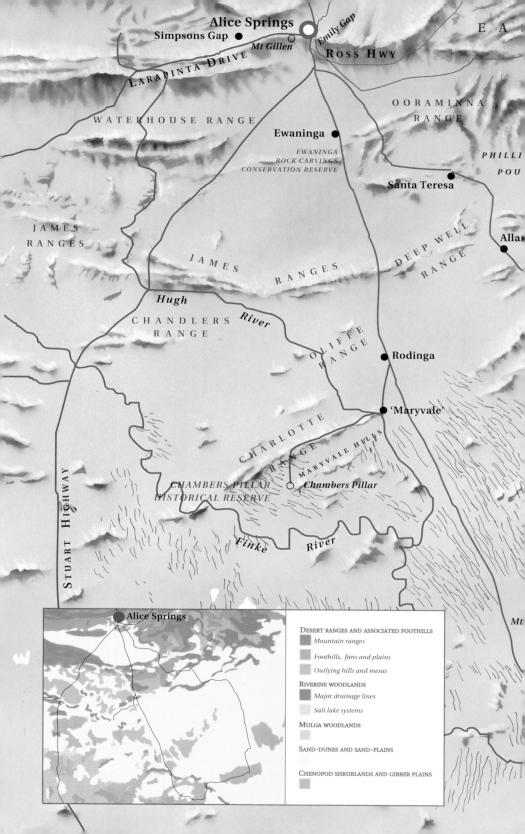

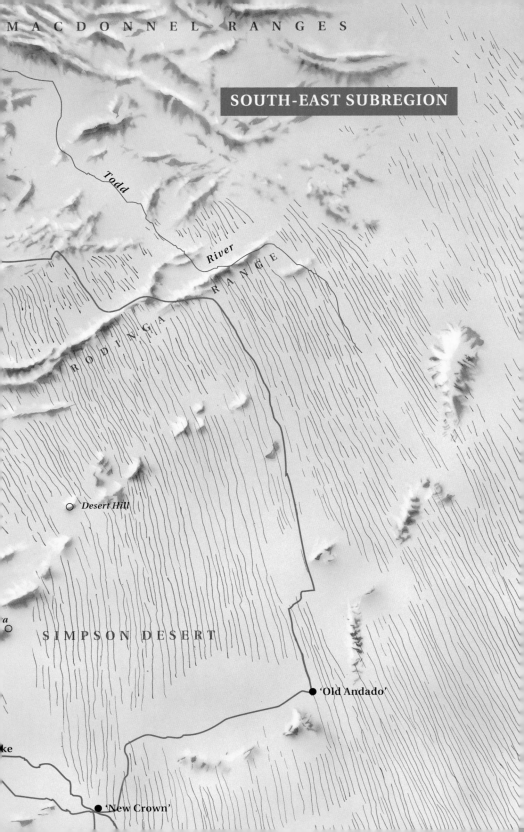

MACDONNEL RANGES

SOUTH-EAST SUBREGION

Todd

River

R O D I N G A   R A N G E

◎ *Desert Hill*

◦ *a*

S I M P S O N   D E S E R T

● 'Old Andado'

ke

● 'New Crown'

Chambers Pillar is a startling pillar of sandstone which stands in the midst of dunes on
the north-west edge of the Simpson Desert.
Explorer John McDouall Stuart named it in
1860. *Friday the 6th of April 1860: "Started
on the same course, 330°, to a remarkable
hill, which has the appearance at this dis-
tance of a locomotive engine with its
funnel...It is a pillar of sandstone, standing
on a hill upwards of one hundred and fifty
feet, quite perpendicular; and it is twenty
feet wide by ten feet deep, with two small
peaks on the top. I have named it
'Chambers Pillar', in honour of James
Chambers, Esq., who, with William Finke,
Esq., has been my great supporter in all my
explorations. To the north and north-east of
it are numerous remarkable hills, which have
a very striking effect in the landscape; they
resemble nothing so much as a number of
old castles in ruin; they are standing in the
midst of sand hills."*

Sand-dunes range from a few
metres to over 30 m high. The eastern
slopes are steeper than the western.
The swale—or trough—between dunes
is not symmetrical; the deepest part

being closest to the western slope (see
Figure 7c). To the east, the slope
increases gradually from the lowest
point of the swale to the base of the
steep uppermost loose-sand zone. Dune
crests are rarely level but have secondary crest features. These secondary
features often involve the development
of a secondary dune as indicated in
Figures 7a and 7b. The hollows between
the main and secondary dune are often
excavated further into deep bowls.
Elsewhere, secondary crest features are
enlarged domes whose summits stand
well above the rest of the crest.

Crests of dunes are usually open
and mobile and bare. In the bowls,
occasional trees, such as *Acacia ligulata*,
A. murrayana and *A. dictyophleba* may
be found. The other crest trees such as
Grevillea stenobotrya and *Gyrostemon
ramulosus* are more common in the
softer sand of the higher areas.

You will see various shapes of
dunes while travelling this route. Some
are shown in Figure 7d.

Figure 8, on the following page,
provides a representative diagram of the
vegetation that you can find on the
dunes in the northern Simpson Desert.

Fig. 7. Sandridge topography

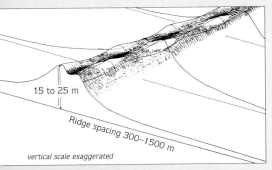

15 to 25 m

Ridge spacing 300–1500 m

vertical scale exaggerated

a. Dune with unidirectional ridges

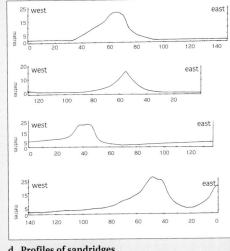

d. Profiles of sandridges

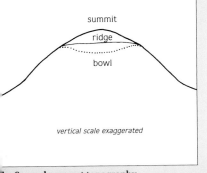

summit

ridge

bowl

vertical scale exaggerated

b. Secondary crest topography

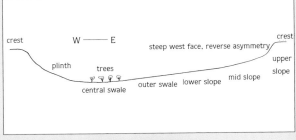

crest   crest

W —— E

steep west face, reverse asymmetry

upper slope

plinth   trees

mid slope

central swale   outer swale lower slope

c. Section through swale showing asymmetry

Adapted from: R. Buckley (1981) 'Soils and vegetation of Central Australian sandridges.' *Aust. J. Ecol.* **6**, 405–422.

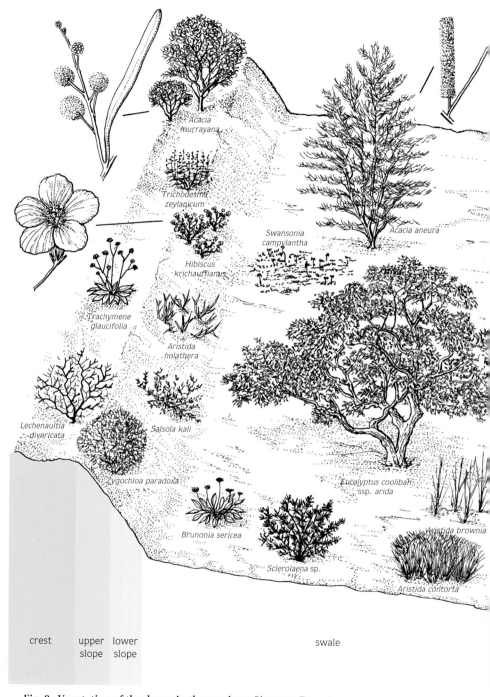

Fig. 8. Vegetation of the dunes in the northern Simpson Desert

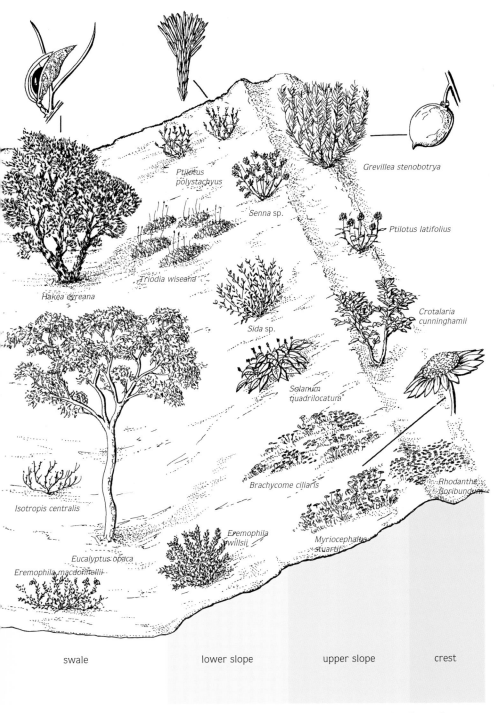

Ptilotus
polystachyus

Grevillea stenobotrya

Senna sp.

Ptilotus latifolius

Triodia wiseana

Hakea eyreana

Sida sp.

Crotalaria
cunninghamii

Solanum
quadrilocatum

Brachycome ciliaris

Rhodanthe
floribundum

Isotropis centralis

Eremophila
willsii

Myriocephalus
stuartii

Eucalyptus opaca

Eremophila macdonnellii

| swale | lower slope | upper slope | crest |

Illustration by Milton Andrews

Rumbulara Land System

On the north-west extremity of the Simpson Desert are the evocative flat-topped hills of the Rumbulara Land System which you can see north of Finke township. The land system extends for about 2400 square km and comprises stony plateaux, up to 60 m high, formed of rock from the Great Artesian Basin which is dissected to show older sandstone beneath. This land system is very sparsely vegetated with Mulga *(Acacia aneura)* over grasses and saltbush and bluebush. Here the Rumbulara Land System abuts the Finke River at Horseshoe Bend.

Gillen Land System

The Gillen Land System of east–west trending ridges is visible returning to Alice Springs via Andado and Santa Theresa.

Endinda Land System

The Endinda Land System of undulating stony plains, sparsely covered with saltbush and bluebush, also occurs in large areas on the northern edges of the Simpson Desert. Good examples of it can be seen near Old Andado Homestead. This barren land system with a few sprigs of saltbush has its own haunting beauty.

PART TWO

HABITATS OF CENTRAL AUSTRALIA

*Why is it that the arid core of the driest habitable
continent in the world is well vegetated? It is quite simply
that Central Australia is not as rainless as other of the
world's deserts. And not nearly as degraded. Unlike the
mobile sand-dunes of the Sahara, even the most arid portion
of Central Australia, the Simpson Desert, receives 100 mm
of average rainfall, enough to provide a light mantle of
vegetation. Most of Central Australia receives around
200 mm of rain on average.*

*Central Australia is, however, a land driven by
extremes, not by averages. Extremes that drive our desert to
do remarkable things such as miraculously transforming
into a garden of flowers after unpredictable,
heavy summer rains.*

*It is in fact rain and the consequent flow of water,
combined with the topography, that largely dictates the
position of the five major habitats of Central Australia: the
desert ranges; the riverine woodlands; the mulga woodlands;
the sand-dunes and sand-plains; and the chenopod
shrublands and gibber plains.*

Desert ranges

Riverine woodlands

Mulga woodland

The Desert Ranges and Associated Foothills, including Outlying Hills

The most reliable thing about rain in arid Australia is its unreliability. Yet reliable water is the single most important factor triggering life in Central Australia. If rain is the orchestral composer of the Australian deserts then topography is the symphonic conductor, redistributing the water that flows across the deceptive uniformity of the inland. In even the flattest environments, water run-off and run-on occurs, creating rich patterns of vegetation and soils—like Aboriginal sand paintings—that you can see from an aircraft.

The ranges, in particular, harvest what water falls and allow for the natural irrigation of plants in these favourable areas at times when the average water availability across the whole landscape would not support growth.

Where water flows, nutrients follow, so that plants with better nutrient status will grow in these naturally irrigated areas; if there are no disturbances like grazing or fire, perennials will gradually dominate. These plants and the animals which live on them will have specific life-history strategies adapted to a relatively favourable and reliable habitat.

The Riverine Woodlands

The rivers and creeks spilling out of the central ranges are themselves ribbons of refuge habitat. The permanent water-tables, small gullies and waterholes along their length provide a reliable habitat for birds, fish and plants. Water supplies can be more reliable either by being continuous, as with permanent watertables; or by being relatively regular, as with run-on areas such as the flanks of the ranges.

The Mulga Woodlands and the Sand-dunes and Sand-plains

Further afield, in the broad sweep of the landscape, water supplies are intermittent and perennials with a greater tolerance for drought, such as Mulga (*Acacia aneura*), will survive on deeper, well-drained soils; and various types of spinifex on skeletal and sandy soils.

Like an old bushman who has lived all his life on damper and salted beef, with few nutrients, mulga and spinifex are tough and wiry and any growth is hard won. If herbivores literally cannot stomach the poor-quality vegetation, for detritivores, particularly termites, it is a banquet. If termites are the grazing ani-

Sand-dunes and sand-plains   Chenopod shrublands

mals of the Mulga woodlands then lizards must be the hunters and it is in these 'poor' areas that we have the greatest diversity of lizards in the world.

The Chenopod Shrublands and Gibber Plains

But while water and nutrients go together, what happens when there are nutrients but no water? In the southern part of Central Australia, along the Lasseter Highway to Uluru (Ayers Rock) and also in the northern Simpson Desert region, the country transforms into one characterised by flat-topped hills or mesas. These are crumbling remnants, 'breakaways', of an even older surface; a flat country becoming flatter. Here, the protective silcrete capping of mesas, now the highest part of the landscape, were originally formed in the lowest part of the landscape, underneath lakes or valleys. The stony or gibber deserts are the scattered scraps of silcrete left after the planing of these already inverted plateaux. The soils of this landscape are nutritionally rich, being formed from swamp, lake and river sediment.

But today these areas are amongst the driest in the continent on which the odd saltbush and bluebush sprout. These plants, although sparse, are nutritionally rich. Rich enough to support small populations of native herbivores so that even the sun- and sand-blasted gibber areas have their own characteristic suite of animals.

It would be hard to imagine an evocative landscape like this cut by Amazon-sized rivers. Yet near a large loop of the Finke River, aptly called Horseshoe Bend, a saltbush flat is bisected by leafy coolibah trees *(Eucalyptus coolibah* ssp. *arida)*. These are the tell-tale signs that an ancient drainage line lies buried beneath. Karinga Creek, just south of Erldunda, is one of many palaeo-drainage channels which once formed vast networks across much of the arid zone. Today some of the interconnected strings of salt lakes and playas, across the arid zone, mark the courses of these fossil rivers. Karinga Creek, for instance, once connected the vast Amadeus salt lake system to the Finke River when that system was a series of large, freshwater lakes. Today this land of mirages is, perhaps deceptively, also a refuge; a rich area in the desert landscape where water and nutrients are pooled.

Above: Fanflower (*Lechenaultia striata*)

Left: Parakeelya (*Calandrinia polyandra*)

Right: Desert Fringe-myrtle (*Calytrix longiflora*)

Right: Desert Fringe-myrtle (*Calytrix longiflora*)

Far right: Tangled Mulla Mulla (*Ptilotus latifolius*)

Below: Cunninghams Rattle-pod (*Crotalaria cunninghamii*)

Above: Desert Rose
(*Gossypium australe*)

Right: Fanflower
(*Lechenaultina striata*)

Below: Minnie Daisy
(*Minuria leptophylla*)

Above: Desert Rose
(*Gossypium australe*)

Right: Bush Hibiscus
(*Radyera farragei*)

Below: Saltspoon Daisy
(*Helipterum stipitatum*)

Above: Bilbies (mother and baby)

Right: Spinifex Hopping-mouse

Above: Crested Pigeon

Below: Nankeen Kestral

Above: Dingo

Above: Feral Camel

Right: Nankeen Kestrals

Below: Dunnart

Above and above right: Barking Spider

Right: Bush Cockroach and egg-sac

Below: Water-holding frog

Above:
Trilling frog

Right: Piedish
Beetle

Below: Centipede

Desert Ranges and Associated Foothills

Introduction

The Central Australian ranges are famous for their pool-sprinkled oases of plants and animals which are protected from evaporation rates as high as 3429 mm. (This is a measure of how much water would evaporate per year, should a body of water be lying around in the Central Australian sun.) Many of the ferns, water plants, cycads and palms and many of the animals of the hidden pools and springs have ancient lineages and you will have to cross thousands of kilometres to the tropical rainforests of New Guinea or the wet sclerophyll forests of Tasmania or even New Zealand to find a close relative. These oases are refuges for many of the rare and relict plants and animals of Central Australia.

The concept of a refuge not only applies to the springs and seepage areas hidden within the ranges, it extends to entire mountain ranges. This is because in this very flat land, any topography will act to funnel and concentrate water. In this environment the desert ranges act as natural irrigation systems. For example, with just, say, 15 mm of rain, the volume of water concentrating in even minor creeks can be 12 to 40 times more than on the surrounding plains.

Where water flows, nutrients will follow, so that in contrast to the broad sweep of the nutritionally poor landscape, uplands (even small rocky outcrops) form islands of nutrient richness. This is one of the few places in Central Australia where water supply is predictable and can be confidently tapped by the roots of plants long after the water reserves in the rest of the landscape have disappeared. As a result, range vegetation is incredibly diverse and will be dominated by perennial plants.

Because the plants are of a better dietary quality, herbivores such as the emu, rock wallaby and even grasshoppers dominate. Birds, in particular, flourish in this landscape of relative plenty.

PLANTS OF THE DESERT RANGES AND ASSOCIATED FOOTHILLS

Upper-storey plants

Genus *Acacia*

Many people think of Australia as the land of the Gum Tree. The reality is that Australia is the land of the wattle or *Acacia*. This is particularly so for Central Australia where one-third of the entire arid zone is covered by *Acacia* shrublands. Acacias belong to the Mimosaceae family. Of the 800 or so Australian species, about 120 occur in Central Australia, with the richest concentration of species occurring in the ranges. In Central Australia, 28 of the 32 endemic species of *Acacia* predominate in the rocky ranges.

Acacia flowers are small and packed together in flower heads which are shaped like balls or spikes. Each flower head can contain up to 100 flowers.

Acacias have pods which often remain on the bush or under it and can be collected to help in identification. The seeds within the pods are on fleshy, often brightly coloured stalks, called arils. To many insects and some birds these are as attractive as a lollipop to a child.

Most Acacias have their leaves replaced by phyllodes after the seedling stage. Phyllodes are flattened leaf-stalks with parallel veins. Phyllodes function as leaves but have reduced pores thereby reducing moisture loss.

silvery tips. The flowers grow in spikes, 1.5 to 3 cm long. The papery pods are short and flat, 1.5 to 5 cm x 0.4 to 1.5 cm.

Acacia aneura (Mulga)

Acacia aneura (Mulga)

Acacia aneura (Mulga)

Mulga occurs in so many different shapes that it can often be difficult to identify. It mostly occurs on the red earth plains surrounding the ranges and looks like an umbrella blown inside-out. On the plains the tree can grow to 15 m. The much smaller, untidy tree that grows on the rocky slopes of the ranges usually has branches growing straight out and grows in stunted, open stands because of the poor water supply in the rocky substrate. The tree often looks grey with

Acacia dictyophleba (Waxy Wattle)

This waxy *Acacia* grows as a shrub up to 3 m high. It can be recognised by the white, waxy patches on its phyllodes. These are narrow and elliptical in shape with dimensions normally 3 to 8.5 cm x 0.4 to 1.5 cm. The veining of the phyllodes

Acacia dictyophleba (Waxy Wattle)

Acacia dictyophleba (Waxy Wattle)

Acacia kempeana (Witchetty Bush)

Acacia georginae (Gidgee)

Acacia georginae (Gidgee)

x 1.2 to 2.5 cm. In humid or rainy weather the tree can give off an unpleasant smell, rather like cat's urine.

Acacia kempeana (Witchetty Bush)

Commonly known as Witchetty Bush because Aboriginal people eat witchetty grubs from the roots, *A. kempeana* grows as a spreading shrub or tree up to 5 m tall. The grey-green phyllodes are narrow and elliptical, 3 to 7.5 cm x 0.4 to 1.5 cm and have rounded ends. The flower-heads are golden spikes about 1 to 2 cm long. The papery pods are flat, about 5 cm x 1 cm.

Acacia macdonnelliensis

This erect, bushy *Acacia* grows up to 5 m tall. The phyllodes are narrow, 6 to 15 cm x 0.1 to 0.3 cm, with fine parallel veins and hooked ends. The flowers which grow straight out from the end of the branches are in large cylindrical spikes 1.5 to 3 cm. The firm, papery pods are narrow, 7.5 cm x 0.2 to 0.4 cm and slightly constricted between seeds.

Acacia tetragonophylla (Dead Finish)

Dead Finish is the common name for this plant because by the time cattle resort to eating its sharp foliage, conditions are just about as bad as they can get—the dead finish. Dead Finish is a straggly bush growing up to 5 m high. Its four-sided,

can best be seen by holding a leaf against the light. The flower-heads are globular and have 30 to 60 flowers. The pods are straight, flat and narrow and about 9 cm long.

Acacia georginae (Gidgee)

This spreading, often straggly tree grows to 5 m. It is often multi-trunked. The tree has a dense crown and offers deep shade. The phyllodes are narrow and tapered toward both ends, 4 to 11 cm x 0.4 to 1.6 cm. The globular flower-head has 12 to 25 flowers. The pods are curved, 6 to 13 cm needle-like phyllodes, 1 to 6 cm x 0.1 cm, end in needle-sharp points. The golden, globular flower-head is densely packed with around 50 flowers. The pods are narrow and twisted and up to 13 cm long. The seeds are surrounded by yellow arils which attract birds and large-bodied ants.

Atalaya hemiglauca (Whitewood)

Whitewood belongs to the Sapindaceae family. The smooth, whitish-grey tree grows to 5 m. The divided leaves have 2 to 6 pairs of long, narrow, leathery leaflets, 6 to 20 cm x 0.8 to 2 cm, which hang down. The bell-shaped, white flowers hang in large clusters. The white, silky petals are oval-shaped, about 0.8 cm x 0.4 cm in size. The hairy fruit consists of two or three winged fruitlets joined together. Each fruitlet is 3 to 4 cm long including the wing.

Acacia tetragonophylla (Dead Finish)

Acacia tetragonophylla (Dead Finish)

Atalaya hemiglauca (Whitewood)

Callitris glaucophylla (White Cypress Pine)

Callitris glaucophylla (White Cypress Pine)

Capparis mitchellii (Wild Orange)

Capparis mitchellii (Wild Orange)

Capparis spinosa (Wild Passionfruit)

Dodonaea viscosa ssp. *mucronata* (Hopbush)

Callitris glaucophylla (White Cypress Pine)

White Cypress Pine is a Gymnosperm or Conifer. Gymnosperms are seed-bearing plants with no true flowers, the reproductive parts are often found in cones. This is one of only two Gymnosperms found in Central Australia. The other one is the cycad, *Macrozamia macdonnelliensis*.

The White Cypress Pine is a small, dark green tree, usually 3 to 4 m high. The tree has small, scale-like, scented leaves which are whorled in threes along the stem. The fruit is a small, globular, woody cone about 2 cm wide.

Capparis mitchellii (Wild Orange)

The Wild Orange belongs to the Capparaceae, or caper, family. Wild Orange develops from a prickly, much-branched shrub into a small tree. As a tree it has a dense canopy which makes it look a little like an orange tree, hence the common

name. The undersides of the oval, leathery leaves, 3 to 6.5 cm long, are like grey felt due to their hairy covering. The large, pale yellow flowers grow in groups of one to four on the end of twigs where each flower grows on its own stem and has fringed petals about 3 cm long. About 120 stamens spray from the flower. The fruit, which grows in the centre of the flower, is globular and hairy and smells strongly when ripe. The flesh between the seeds is edible.

Capparis spinosa (Wild Passionfruit)

Like its close relative, Wild Orange, Wild Passionfruit is a member of the caper family and not a passion-fruit at all. In fact, the capers you buy in a jar are the pickled buds of the Mediterranean variety of *C. spinosa*. Wild Passionfruit grows as a sprawling shrub to 4 m in diameter. The hairless, leathery leaves are oval with pointed ends, a

hooked tip and two spines at the base. The solitary, large, white flowers grow on their own stalk. They have four white petals, about 2 cm long and numerous long, white stamens spray outward. The flowers open at sunset and fall off about 15 hours later. The ovary develops into an elliptical fruit about 4 cm long, red or yellow and splitting when ripe. The pith is yellow and has large, black, inedible seeds. The fruit is edible.

Dodonaea viscosa ssp. *mucronata* (Hopbush)

Hopbush belongs to the family Sapindaceae. The Hopbush is a small, rounded shrub up to 2 m high. The shiny green leaves are oval to spade-shaped, 2.5 to 6.5 cm x 1.0 to 2.5 cm, with wavy margins. The leaves are waxy, giving the plant a shiny appearance. The orange fruit capsule has three to four wings, each about 0.5 cm wide. The capsule is about 2 cm long.

Genus *Eremophila*

Eremophilas belong to the Myoporaceae family. The common name for *Eremophila* is 'desert fuchsia', even though they are not related to the garden fuchsia plant. 'Eremophila' means desert-loving and it is indeed in the arid zone that they have come into their own. The genus *Eremophila* is living proof that evolution is a dynamic process since, in the Pilbara region of Western Australia, it is currently undergoing rapid evolution into a series of complexes and intergrades. Currently there are 180 species. In Central Australia there are about 28 species.

Eremophilas are shrubs up to 2 m high. In flower they are covered with pretty, bell-shaped flowers in colours ranging from white to lilac, purple, blue, green, yellow, orange, red and carmine.

Not surprising for desert lovers, Eremophilas cope well with drought. When times get tough, they drop their leaves. They have very hard seed cases which can lie dormant for many years, responding well after fire and rain.

Eremophila freelingii (Rock Fuchsia)

Eremophila freelingii (Rock Fuchsia)

Often looking more dead than alive, these 1 to 2 m high bushes have hairy, greyish, narrow, aromatic leaves, 3 to 8 cm x 0.3 to 1 cm, which can often be waxy. The tubular flower has flaring lobes. The flower is usually lilac but can be pink, blue or even white. The ovoid, 0.6 to 0.8 cm long fruit is glandular and hairy.

Eremophila latrobei (Latrobe's Desert Fuchsia)

This 1 to 3 m high bush is most easily recognised when in flower when it is covered with bright red flowers. The leaves vary from narrow, green and almost hairless, to wider, hairy and grey-green, 1 to 8 cm x 0.5 to 5 cm. The conical fruit is 5 to 10 cm long.

Eremophila longifolia (Weeping Emu Bush)

This shrub to small tree, 1 to 6 m high, has weeping branches. The dull green

Eremophila freelingii (Rock Fuchsia)

Eremophila latrobei
(Latrobe's Desert Fuchsia)

leaves are narrow and up to 15 cm long, normally sparsely haired. One to three brick red, spotted flowers grow out of the leaf axils. There is an obvious knob at the base of the flowers. The fleshy fruit becomes purple when ripe and is a favoured food of Emus.

Eremophila latrobei
(Latrobe's Desert Fuchsia)

Eremophila longifolia
(Weeping Emu Bush)

Genus *Eucalyptus*

Eucalypts belong to the Myrtaceae family, along with the bottlebrush, teatrees and paperbarks. Eucalypts can be trees or shrubs. They secrete a resinous gum, hence the common name Gum Tree. Mallees are a growth-form rather than a particular species, that is, a *Eucalpytus* that has many trunks arising from the same root or lignotuber. The leaves of Eucalypts are different shapes and sizes at different ages of the tree. Young trees have mostly opposite leaves whereas adult trees have mostly alternate leaves. The flower is in a woody cup, commonly called the gumnut. The cap of the gumnut or flower bud is really the fused petals and sepals and this drops off when flowering occurs, releasing the stamens which spray out from a ring at the top of the cup. The fruit is a woody capsule.

Eucalyptus gamophylla
(Blue Mallee)

A mallee which is mostly 3 to 6 m high. The bark is smooth and white or grey coloured. The adult leaves are blue-green in colour and are oval, about 6 to 8 cm x 1 to 1.5 cm and joined in pairs, encircling the stem. The buds occur in clusters of three to seven and the flowers are cream. The small gumnuts, about

81

Eucalyptus gamophylla (Blue Mallee)

Eucalyptus gamophylla
(Blue Mallee)

Eucalyptus papuana (Ghost Gum)

The Ghost Gum is one of the Centre's most distinctive Eucalypts, its beautiful white trunk almost shimmering against the red rock on which it often grows. The Ghost Gum is a tree, 5 to 15 m high, but sometimes growing to 20 m. Its adult long, narrow leaves, 5 to 18 cm x 1.2 to 4.5 cm, hang down in clusters on drooping branchlets. The buds are in clusters of five to eleven, developing into cream flowers. The

Eucalyptus gamophylla (Blue Mallee)

0.5 to 0.7 cm, are cyclindrical, tapering to the base. The valves are at or below the rim.

large, pink, stalked gumnuts are oval-shaped, almost urn-like, 2 to 2.5 cm wide, with the valves inside.

gumnuts are small and cylindrical, 0.7 to 1 cm x 0.6 to 0.9 cm, with valves inside.

Eucalyptus opaca (Bloodwood)

Bloodwoods have tessellated or pavement-like bark. They are usually trees 6 to 11 m tall, sometimes taller. The dull green adult leaves are not opposite and are long and narrow, 10 to 15 cm x 1 to 2 cm. The buds are in clusters of three to seven, developing into cream flowers. The

Eucalyptus papuana (Ghost Gum)

Eucalyptus opaca (Bloodwood)

Eucalyptus opaca (Bloodwood)

Eucalyptus opaca (Bloodwood)

Eucalyptus sessilis (Finke River Mallee)

This straggly mallee is 2 to 4 m high. It has smooth, brown-grey bark shedding in strips around its lower trunk. The fresh bark is smooth white or light grey. The dull, grey-green leaves are long ovals 8 to 19 cm x 2 to 4.5 cm. The buds grow in clusters of three to seven, developing into yellow or cream flowers. The fruits are globular, 1.4 to 2.1 cm x 1.6 to 2 cm, the most distinctive thing about them being that they have no stalks, growing flush against the stem. Its common name reflects the fact that it is found, amongst other places, on the sand-stone hills overlooking the Finke.

Ficus platypoda (Native Fig)

The figs clinging to the rocks in gullies of the central ranges, their roots seeming to suck moisture from rock, are remnants of an ancient rainforest environment. This many-stemmed, sprawling shrub has shiny, dark green leaves about

Ficus platypoda (Native Fig)

Eucalyptus papuana (Ghost Gum)

Hakea suberea
(Corkwood)

Ficus platypoda (Native Fig)

9 cm x 3 cm. The edible
fruits or figs turn from
orange to red to purple as
they ripen. The flowers are
contained within the inner
walls of the fig. The fig is

Hakea suberea (Corkwood)

called a false fruit
because it is really the
fleshy swollen end of the
stem, surrounding the
flowers.

Hakea suberea
(Corkwood)

Corkwood belongs to the
Proteaceae family. Only
two genera in this big
family are represented
in Central Australia,
Hakea and *Grevillea*.
Corkwood is a small,
gnarled tree, up to 6 m
tall, with thick, corky
bark, deeply fissured.
The long, narrow leaves,
up to 30 cm, are circular
in cross-section. The
cream flowers grow in
clusters up to 12 cm long.
The woody fruit is oval-
shaped, often swollen in
the lower half and with a
beaked end. The seed is
winged.

Pittosporum
phylliraeoides
(Weeping Pittosporum)

This small, weeping tree,
up to 10 m tall, belongs to

Hakea suberea (Corkwood)

the Pittosporaceae, or
sticky seed, family. The
long leaves, 2 to 10 cm x
0.2 to 1 cm, hang on pen-
dulous branches. The
solitary flowers are small,
cream bells, 0.7 to 0.9 cm
long. The round seed cap-
sules are bright orange
and about 1 to 2 cm in
size. The capsules split
open to show the seeds
enveloped in a sticky, red
pulp.

Pittosporum phylliraeoides
(Weeping Pittosporum)

Pittosporum phylliraeoides
(Weeping Pittosporum)

Pandorea doratoxylon
(Spearbush)

Spearbush belongs to the
Bignoniaceae family. It is a
many-stemmed shrub
growing up to 4 m, found
only in gorges and on sheltered hillsides amongst
rocks. The leaves are

Rhagodia eremaea
(Ruby Saltbush)

Rhagodia eremaea
(Ruby Saltbush)

Rhagodia eremaea
(Ruby Saltbush)

85

Pandorea doratoxylon (Spearbush)

Ventilago viminalis
(Supplejack)

Pandorea doratoxylon (Spearbush)

divided into five to nine leaflets, each about 1.5 to 4 cm long. The clustered flowers are large, cream, lobed bells with brown-purple markings in the throat which is also densely hairy. The fruit is a capsule about 10 cm long. The stems of the Spearbush form long canes which are used by Aboriginal people for making spears.

Rhagodia eremaea
(Ruby Saltbush)

R. eremaea belongs to the saltbush or Chenopodiaceae family. It is a rounded shrub up to 2 m high. The leaves are wide and flat, 1 to 2 cm long and have a mealy covering below. The fruit is a red berry about 0.3 cm wide.

Ventilago viminalis
(Supplejack)

Supplejack belongs to the Rhamnaceae family and can best be recognised by its characteristic intertwining trunks. These are covered by rough, flaky, grey-brown bark. The long, narrow leaves, 5 to 15 cm x 0.6 to 1.2 cm, hang down. The underside of the leaves are whitish. The tiny green to cream-yellow flowers develop into globular nut-like fruits with a leathery wing 2 to 4 cm long.

Ventilago viminalis
(Supplejack)

Ground-storey plants

Aristida contorta
(Bunched Kerosene Grass)

Bunched Kerosene Grass is a semi-erect annual or short-lived perennial grass reaching 30 cm in height. The leaf blades are tightly

Aristida contorta
(Bunched Kerosene Grass)

rolled, tending to curl on drying. Aristidas are readily recognised by their characteristic spear-like seeds, which have a hairy, pointed base and three spreading awns which act to drive the seed into the ground. In *A. contorta* the three-awn has a twisted column 1 to 4 cm long and unequal branches up to 6 cm long.

Aristida contorta
(Bunched Kerosene Grass)

Calotis hispidula
(Bogan Flea)

The genus *Calotis*, which is endemic to Australia, belongs to the Compositae family. Bogan Flea is a daisy, about 5 to 15 cm high. Like all Calotis species, the seed-head of this pretty little daisy develops into a horrible burr. Each seed in the

Cheilanthes lasiophylla
(Woolly Cloak-fern)

Cheilanthes lasiophylla (Woolly Cloak-fern)

seed-head has a crown of
five to six spreading spines
which are extremely persistent.

Cheilanthes lasiophylla
(Woolly Cloak-fern)

Ferns have no seeds or
flowers and their complex
sex-life involves spores
which must have free water
for the transfer of gametes
in the sexual stage. Ferns
are therefore found at the
bottom of rocky gorges or
in other places which flood.
The Woolly Cloak-fern is a
rockfern and as the name
suggests is ubiquitous in
rocky situations. The blue-
green fronds are densely

Enchylaena tomentosa
(Ruby Saltbush)

clustered, about 15 cm long and divided into many lobes. The fronds are hairy, the hair forming a thick, golden-brown cloak on the back of the leaves.

Enchylaena tomentosa (Ruby Saltbush)

Ruby Saltbush, as the name suggests, belongs to the Chenopodiaceae, or salt-bush, family. Ruby Saltbush is a straggling, small shrub which grows to 1 m high. Its slender leaves are suc-culent, 0.8 to 2 cm long and covered with fine, downy hair which extends to the stems. The tiny flow-ers are hard to see but the fleshy, red, 0.5 cm wide fruits or berries make this plant easy to identify. The fleshy parts of the fruits are edible.

Hybanthus aurantiacus
(Orange Spade Flower)

Hybanthus aurantiacus
(Orange Spade Flower)

Hybanthus aurantiacus (Orange Spade Flower)

The Orange Spade Flower belongs to the Violaceae, or violet, family. This perennial herb has a golden-orange spade-shaped flower. The four upper petals are very small and the lower petal is large and shaped like a spade. The 4 cm long leaves are flat, narrow and toothed. The fruit is a cap-sule, 0.5 to 0.9 cm long.

89

Indigofera leucotricha
(White Indigo)

the white-grey bush often seen on hillsides in company with Eremophilas. The bush is covered with whitish hair which gives it the whitish appearance. The compound leaf has around 20 leaflets. The flower has five petals. The back petal stands erect, the two lowest petals join to form the 'keel', the two side petals forming wings. The red flowers are born on a spike 3 to 6 cm long.

Ptilotus obovatus
(Silvertails)

Silvertails belong to the Amaranthaceae family, commonly known as pussy-tails. The Silvertail is a little shrub 10 to 130 cm tall and across. The flowers are gathered together to form fluffy heads, or 'pussytails'. The flower spikes are hemi-spherical and usually 1 to 3 cm long, pale pink and covered with snow-white hairs.

Senna artemisioides ssp. *artemisioides* (Silver Senna)

Senna artemisioides
ssp. *artemisioides*
(Silver Senna)

This silver shrub of the Caesalpiniaceae family is from 1 to 2 m high. The grey to green leaves, 3 to 6 cm long, are divided into leaflets of three to ten pairs. The silvery colour is due to the white, flattened

Indigofera leucotricha
(White Indigo)

Indigofera leucotricha belongs to the Fabaceae family; the family of keeled pea-flowers. Like the Acacias and Sennas, plants of this family are also legumes with the seeds encased in a pod, or legume. *I. leucotricha* is a small, erect shrub which grows up to 1 m high. It is

90

Themeda triandra
(Kangaroo Grass)

hairs on the leaves. The flowers are sweetly scented, globular cups which grow in a cluster. The rounded petals are 0.7 to 1 cm x 0.5 to 0.7 cm in size. The flat, oblong pod, 4 to 8 cm x 0.6 to 1 cm, is sometimes a shining brown colour.

Ptilotus obovatus
(Silvertails)

Themeda triandra
(Kangaroo Grass)

As is obvious from the common name, Kangaroo Grass belongs to the Poaceae, or grass, family. This densely tufted, leafy perennial grows up to 90 cm high in tussocks up to 22 cm wide. The plants are highly coloured from pale green during growth to reddish-brown at maturity. The stems are undivided and have two to six nodes which are powdery. The leaves, or blades, are flat, or loosely folded and tapering.

Spinifex (*Triodia* and *Plectrachne* genera)

If one plant characterises Central Australia it is spinifex. Not to be confused with the true *Spinifex* genus of the coastal sand-dunes, this magnificent grass is uniquely Australian. But beware when you introduce yourself to a spinifex clump, since it has a very prickly personality. There are about 30 different species in the two genera. The most common are often categorised as either 'hard' or 'soft', depending literally, on whether you can grab a handful without puncturing yourself. Most spinifexes have localised distributions, with those in the desert ranges, such as the MacDonnells, having the greatest number of species.

Triodia clelandii (Weeping Spinifex)

Weeping Spinifex, like all spinifexes, belong the Poaceae, or grass, family. Weeping Spinifex forms compact, hemispherical tussocks, 30 to 60 cm high and 90 to 120 cm wide. The stems are erect, rigid, smooth and hairless. The leaves have prominent soft, tangled, woolly hairs at the base and sometimes on the lower part of the leaf. The blades, 5 to 14 cm long, are slender and rigid forming firm sharp points and are dark green when young. The seed-head droops and nods to one side. Weeping Spinifex is common in the MacDonnell Ranges.

Triodia clelandii (Weeping Spinifex)

Spinifex plains

Triodia irritans
(Porcupine Spinifex)

Triodia irritans forms compact tussocks up to 60 cm high and 90 to 120 cm wide but often much smaller. The stems are strongly branched at the upper nodes. The blades, 7 to 22 cm long, are slender but rigid and needle-like, with fine but firm, sharp points, greyish or bluish-green in colour and hairless and smooth. It occurs on sandstone and quartzite rocks, in rugged places such as at Kata Tjuta (The Olgas).

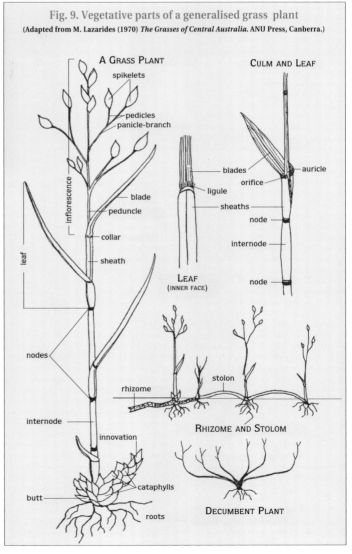

Fig. 9. Vegetative parts of a generalised grass plant
(Adapted from M. Lazarides (1970) *The Grasses of Central Australia*. ANU Press, Canberra.)

A GRASS PLANT
- spikelets
- pedicles
- panicle-branch
- inflorescence
- blade
- peduncle
- collar
- sheath
- leaf
- nodes
- internode
- innovation
- butt
- cataphylls
- roots

CULM AND LEAF
- blades
- auricle
- orifice
- ligule
- sheaths
- node
- internode
- node

LEAF
(INNER FACE)

RHIZOME AND STOLOM
- rhizome
- stolon

DECUMBENT PLANT

Triodia irritans
(Porcupine Spinifex)

Amyema miquelii
(Mistletoe)

Amyema miquelii (Mistletoe)

Amyema miquelii belongs to the Mistletoe family, Loranthaceae. Mistletoes are parasitic shrubs which are attached to a host tree's branches from which it gains its nutrients and water. Mistletoes are fairly common on trees in Central Australia. *A. miquelii* is frequently found on Eucalypts. The hairless, 4 to 28 cm long leaves often look a coppery colour. The red flowers are stalked and grow in clusters of three. The fruit is cylindrical to pear-shaped, 0.8 to 1.2 cm long. Like other mistletoes,

Tripogon loliiformis (Five-minute Grass)

This grass is a slender annual, rarely over 15 cm high. It forms compact leafy tufts with dense, fibrous butts. The leaf blades are 5 to 7.5 cm long, narrow, flat or loosely folded and finely pointed and mainly occur at the base of the plant. The seed-head is a spike 5 to 8 cm long and up to 0.5 cm wide, erect and pale or olive green. Found throughout the region but particularly on stony tablelands and alluvial areas. The common name of the plant is a reflection of the plant's fast growth after only a little rain.

Tripogon loliiformis
(Five-minute Grass)

PLANTS FOUND ON DOLOMITE

Dolomite is a rock similar to limestone. It is dark grey in colour. The rock becomes plastic under pressure and during the building of the MacDonnell Ranges, this rock was squeezed into spectacular shapes. Dolomite is common in the East and West MacDonnell Ranges and is common along the road. Some of the plants that you are likely to see on dolomite are described here.

the fruit is a great favourite of birds which distribute the seeds to other trees.

Eucalyptus eucentrica (Limestone Mallee)

See page 73 for a brief description of the genus *Eucalyptus*

The Limestone Mallee is 2 to 9 m high. The bark is smooth and pale grey, though at the base it is rough. The adult leaves, 6 to 9 cm x 1.2 to 2 cm are alternate and the same dull grey-green colour top and bottom. The flowers form clusters of 7 to 15 buds which have long, pointed caps. The flowers are white or cream. The globular, woody fruits, 0.5 to 0.8 cm x 0.5 to 0.8 cm, have protruding valves and are on stalks. Limestone Mallee is named after the habitat in which it occurs.

Triodia longiceps (Giant Grey Spinifex)

See also page 84.

This spinifex is one to be wary of. It grows in enor-mous, unfriendly tussocks up to 2.4 m high and 2 m wide. Its thick, rigid stems are hairless, smooth, strongly branched from the lower nodes and purple when young. The leaf blades are extremely rigid, with hard, sharp, needle-like points, 10 to 25 cm long or more! This magnificent plant is probably the largest and coarsest spinifex in Australia.

Triodia longiceps (Giant Grey Spinifex)

Eucalyptus eucentrica (Limestone Mallee)

Because the plants in these better-watered areas are of better dietary quality, animals that require a constant supply of good quality food such as herbivores (for example, wallabies) and birds dominate. Unlike the broad-sweep habitats of the plains where most of the birds are nomadic, most birds of the ranges are sedentary. In particular honeyeaters, parrots (see Chapter six, Riverine Woodlands), pigeons and grass finches depend on daily drinks of water (more than half the desert-dwelling birds appear not to need water at all). The bird illustrations in this book are courtesy of Peter Slater.

Birds

Pigeons

Common Bronzewing
Phaps chalcoptera

A large, 33 cm, plump pigeon with extensive bronze on the wing. The upper parts of the bird are brown with pale margins of feathers giving a bold, scaly appearance. There is a conspicuous curving white line leading back from the bill under the eye and a little down the side of the neck. The breast is a pinkish grey. The female is duller than the male. Common Bronzewings are usually found in pairs though occasionally they'll gather in small flocks. They fly with swift, steady wing-beats close to the ground, though they prefer to walk short distances feeding mostly on seeds. The voice is a penetrating and mournful 'oom...oom'.

Crested Pigeon
Ocyphaps lophotes

The Crested Pigeon is a grey pigeon, about 33 cm long, with a slender, black crest. The wings have fine, wavy, black bars. It occurs singly, in pairs or even parties. Its flight is swift in bursts of whistling wing-beats or single wing-beats interrupted with long glides. When landing it swings its tail high above the body. Its voice is a surprised 'woop!'. It prefers lightly wooded country where water is present. A ground-feeder, it eats little else but seeds.

Common Bronzewing
Phaps chalcoptera

Spinifex Pigeon
Petrophassa plumifera

A plump, erect, ruddy-buff pigeon, about 22 cm long. It has a very tall, erect, sandy crest, wavy, black barrings on the wings and prominent facial patterns. Underparts are white or buff-white in colour. The Spinifex Pigeon is usually found in small groups of around 15 birds. They run and dodge swiftly through spinifex and over rocks where they feed on the seeds dropped in-between

plants. They fly fast and low over the ground with bursts of rapid wing-beats alternating with gliding on downswept wings. The voice is a soft 'cooroo-coo'; 'coo'; or hoarse 'coorr'.

Diamond Dove
Geopelia cuneata

At about 20 cm this is the smallest member of the pigeon family. It is a diminutive blue-grey dove, washed smoky brown above with a red eyering and scattered, fine white spots on the wings. The Diamond Dove spends much of its time on the ground feeding on small seeds, though it will eat green matter and even insects in some seasons. It can run very fast. Its flight is swift and direct and has a swooping charac-

Spinifex Pigeon
Petrophassa plumifera

Bronze-Cuckoo uses the nests of fairy-wrens, thorn-bills and gerygones as its main host. The bird is an insect- and caterpillar-eater hunting by a perch-and-pounce technique. It has a mournful, descending whistle which is often repeated.

Mistletoebird
Dicaeum hirundinaceum

ter when the bird closes its wings for a moment. Diamond Doves move in large numbers from place to place looking for food. The voice is a sad, mournful 'coo-oo...coo-oo'.

Cuckoos

Pallid Cuckoo
Cuculus pallidus

A graceful, longish-tailed grey cuckoo, 30 to 33 cm, with a curving, dark line through its eye and white mark on the back of the head and at the shoulder. Its flight-feathers are notched and spotted white and the tail is prominently notched and whitish. Many birds play unwitting host to the egg and young of the Pallid Cuckoo, which ejects the eggs and young of the host. The most commonly parasitised nests in the Centre are cup-shaped nests like those of the honeyeaters, particularly the Singing Honeyeater and the White-plumed Honeyeater. Solitary birds, Pallid Cuckoos feed on hairy caterpillars, grasshoppers and beetles, flying from

branch to branch. The sustained flight is swift and direct and slightly undulating. The voice is a melancholy ascending scale of eight notes; also a demented 'crookyer, crookyer...' in pursuit of females. The female, on the other hand, has one harsh, single call.

Horsfield's Bronze-cuckoo
Chrysococcyx basalis

This is a dull coloured bronze-cuckoo, about 17 cm, with a brown head and bronze upperparts which are glossy green in sunlight. The breast is dull white with dull brown bars. A solitary bird which shifts north in winter, the Horsfield's

Horsfield's Bronze-cuckoo
Chrysococcyx basalis

Mistletoebird *Dicaeum hirundinaceum* (male)

A tiny bird, 10 cm, the male is brightly coloured, glossy blue-black above with the chest, throat and under the base of the tail a bright scarlet. The female is grey above with whitish underparts. The base of her tail is a pale, washed red. The Mistletoebird has a specialised diet of the sticky mistletoe fruit, though it will take other fruit and insects occasionally. Mistletoebirds forage along mistletoe, flying from one clump to the next in a high, bullet-like flight. The call is a high-pitched, sharp, whistled 'szit' or 'dzee' in contact with other birds. It also has a distinctive song which involves two or three rising and falling whistling notes, 'wait-a-bit, wait-a-bit'. The bird is also a mimic.

Mistletoebird *Dicaeum hirundinaceum* (female)

Red-backed Kingfisher
Halcyon pyrrhopygia

These little kingfishers, 20 to 24 cm, are better adapted to the desert than any of their relatives and can live far from water. The Red-backed Kingfisher is paler than the Sacred Kingfisher. The male has a whitish crown, streaked grey-green, with wings and tail a dusty pale blue. The back and rump is orange-tan and whitish below. The female is duller and greyer above. Red-backed Kingfishers

Red-backed Kingfisher
Halcyon pyrrhopygia

usually live in loose groups of four or five, or in pairs. They can often be solitary. They eat reptiles, insects, even young birds. Like all kingfishers, it sits motionless on a branch, staring down and waiting for prey. Flight is swift and direct. The voice is a mournful 'peel' whistle, repeated monotonously.

Rainbow Bee-eater
Merops ornatus

Australia's only Bee-eater, this is a gorgeous, pale-green and blue bird, 23 cm,

Rainbow Bee-eater
Merops ornatus

of graceful flight. It has a fine-curved black bill, blue-edged, black eyemark and a pale orange throat with a black mark in the centre. The male's two central tail-feathers extend 25 to 50 mm as wires. The female has shorter tail feathers. These birds are communal, travelling in groups of 20 or 30. They are also migratory, moving into Central Australia to breed in spring and then moving north during March–April to winter as far north as New Guinea and

into Indonesia. Rainbow Bee-eaters catch food on the wing, sallying forth from a branch. They eat flying insects including wasps and bees. They are elegant, acrobatic fliers with broad but pointed wings. Their voice is a melodious 'trrrp, trrrp', usually on the wing.

Richard's Pipit
Anthus novaeseelandiae

This is a familiar, slender, streaked brownish bird, 15 to 17 cm, with a slender pale brown bill and long, pale pinkish-brown legs. Richard's Pipit is a wide-ranging bird from Africa, Europe and Indonesia to Australia and New Zealand. In Central Australia it prefers bare ground interspersed with spare patches of cover. It runs along the ground to feed, picking up small grasshoppers, ants, caterpillars, beetles and other insects, occasionally even seeds. When it isn't running, it wags its tail up and down, hinting that the bird is in fact related to the wagtail family. Its flight is fluttering with the tail often spread and depressed. Its voice is a repeated, trilled 'peer' in flight.

Rufous Songlark
Cinclorhamphus mathewsi

Living up to its name, the male, during breeding season, sings a rich, metallic

Rufous Songlark
Cinclorhamphus mathewsi

throat grading rapidly into white below. It is found in pairs to family groups, foraging on insects, fruits and even nestling birds. Their flight is of long, graceful undulations and when they land they have the characteristic habit of repeatedly refolding their wings, hence their other common name 'shufflew-reel'. Looking like a Richard's Pipit, but in fact unrelated, the tawny rump seen in flight is the best field mark to distinguish it. The bird flies in dashing, looping undulations and eats insects, small vertebrates and plant matter. The male song is very sweet and has an almost ventriloquial quality. It often begins with a clear, loud trill, then develops into a full refrain, 'wit-cher wit-cher-witchy-weedle', often with a whip-like effect on the first syllable.

Cuckoo-shrikes

Black-faced Cuckoo-shrike
Coracina novaehollandiae

Neither cuckoo nor shrike, the cuckoo-shrikes take their name from their cuckoo-like form and shrike-like bill. The Black-faced Cuckoo-shrike is a widespread and familiar bird, about 33 cm. It is smoky-grey with a distinctive black face and

BRUCE THOMSON

Black-faced Cuckoo-shrike
Coracina novaehollandiae

ing'. The voice is a plaintive 'plee-urk' or a pleasant chirring.

Ground Cuckoo-shrike
Coracina maxima

This slender and long-legged cuckoo-shrike, 36 cm, is slightly bigger than the Black-faced Cuckoo-shrike and is adapted to feeding on the ground. Its head and upper body are pale grey; and its wings and long, slightly forked, tail are black, contrasting with the finely barred white underparts, lower back and rump. Its eye is pale. On the ground groups of three to seven birds forage for grasshoppers, beetles and other insects, occasionally leaping into the air to catch an insect. In flight they show a deeply forked tail. During flight they constantly call a high pitched and loud 'kree-el' or 'cheer-cheer...kee-lick, kee-lick'.

Robins

Hooded Robin
Melanodryas cucullata

This 14 to 17 cm solid and sedentary robin is the most widespread of Australian robins. The male has a distinctive black hood which forms a wedge-shape on its white breast and it has prominent, white bars on its shoulder and wing. Where the male is black, the female is grey-brown. Established pairs keep to their territory year round. Mostly they sit hunched quietly in a tree waiting for prey on the ground on which to pounce. They join the pre-dawn chorus with a metallic 'peet...peet...peet'.

Red-capped Robin
Petroica goodenovii

One of the most brightly coloured robins, it is about 11 cm. The male is unmistakable with his brilliant scarlet cap and breast; black above with a bold

Hooded Robin
Melanodryas cucullata

white wing-slash and white edges to the tail. The female is brown with a faint pink flush on the forehead. Largely solitary, the bird forages by perch-and-pounce, perching on a low branch about a metre off the ground and pouncing on grasshoppers, bugs, beetles, flies, moths, ants and small mantids. The male's song is a reeling, metallic 'trr-trr-der-radeedee'. Both sexes communicate to each other by a 'toc-toc' sound, somewhat like tapping stones.

Red-capped Robin
Petroica goodenovii

Rufous Whistler
Pachycephala rufiventris

There is scarcely a tract of open forest anywhere without a Rufous Whistler. About 17 cm, the male is grey above with a blackish mask extending down the side of the neck and joining like a broad necklace separating the white throat from the rufous underparts. The female is brownish-grey above and pale buff below with dark streaks. Occurring mostly alone or in pairs, the birds hop methodically from branch to branch taking insects and larvae and occasionally berries. The voice is a loud, vigorous 'ee-chong, joey-joey' often heard after a loud noise, like slamming a car door; it also calls a plaintive 'sweet'.

Rufous Whistler
Pachycephala rufiventris
(male, above, and female)

Grey Fantail
Rhipidura fuliginosa

A small, 16 cm, active, grey fantail with extensive white in the tail feathers. The Grey Fantail, more than other fantails, flies twisting and turning so as to pick up a range of flying insects from mid-air. Never still, the birds spiral up and down tree trunks and zigzag out along branches often voicing a 'dek'. During breeding the song develops into a tinny, sweet, ascending series of short notes with a twangy, whistled quality, obvious in the dawn chorus.

Babblers

Grey-crowned Babbler
Pomatostomus temporalis

Babblers are amongst the most delightful of birds. They go around in groups of about 12, noisy and gregarious, bounding along the

ground or flying in a follow-the-leader fashion. The Grey-crowned Babbler is the larger of the babblers, about 25 cm. It has very large, white eyebrows, bordering a narrow, pale grey crown. The eye is pale yellow. The group forages on the ground probing under rocks and into the soil and leaf-litter with long, curved bills, for spiders, insects and lizards. They also forage in bushes and trees. Groups of babblers are incessant, fussy chatterers. They can call a clear 'yahoo' or brisk 'gowahee, gowahee, gowahee' and also strident 'peeoo peeoo peeoo'.

White-browed Babbler
Pomatostomus superciliosus

This smaller babbler, about 20 cm, is a duller brown and its white eyebrow is relatively smaller than the Grey-crowned Babbler and its crown is dark brown. Other than these differences its habits are much the same including the cacophony of sound that accompanies the group.

Zebra Finch
Poephila guttata

At 10 cm this is the smallest finch in Australia. It is also the most widespread. They are stocky, grey little birds with red-orange bills. The male has a vertical white and dark streak on its face, an orange-tan cheek-patch and orange-tan flanks which are spotted white. The tail is blackish, barred white. Zebra Finches are social birds, living in close-knit flocks of 10 to 100 or more year round. They feed in flocks on the ground. The Zebra Finch call is a distinctive 'tya...tya...tya'. Large flocks make a blizzard of these calls, heard quite some distance off. Zebra Finches, being mainly seed-eaters, need to drink water regularly.

Painted Firetail
Emblema picta

A colourful finch with a bright red rump, about 10 cm, it has an unfinch-like pointed, partly red bill. The bird has a

Painted Firetail
Emblema picta

distinctive colouration: brown above, black below, heavily spotted white and set off by a brilliant scarlet face and throat and red patch on the centre of the breast. Among the gorges, the bird establishes small, loose, sedentary groups of 5 to 30 birds. Fallen grass seeds are the staple diet. The voice is a harsh 'trut' or 'check, check', also a wheezy 'che-che-che-che-che-che, werreeeee-oweeeeee'.

Fairy-wrens

Splendid Fairy-wren
Malurus splendens

A pretty, 14 cm bird, the male is a brilliant blue or purplish-blue with a black band across the breast and nape of neck. The female is brown with a bright blue tail and chestnut patch around the eye. The Splendid Fairy-wren lives and breeds in small groups with helpers to attend the nest. They are sedentary. Their diet is insects, larvae and other invertebrates including spi-

ders. They feed hopping on the ground or dashing between bushes. The voice is a soft 'trrrrp', 'treeee' and also a rich, gushing reel.

Variegated Fairy-wren
Malurus assimilis

A red-shouldered fairy-wren, about 14 cm, the male has a jet black throat and upper breast and a deep lilac-blue back and chestnut to brick-red shoulder. The female is brown above and fawn below, the tail a washed blue. The Variegated Fairy-wren has the same habits as the Splendid Fairy-wren. It has a broader bill than the Splendid Fairy-wren and is more of a generalist, even eating occasional fruits. Its voice is similar to the Splendid's but more high-pitched.

Splendid Fairy-wren
Malurus splendens
(female, above, and male)

101

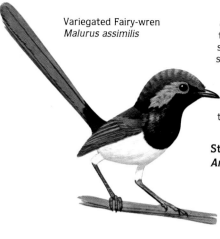

Variegated Fairy-wren
Malurus assimilis

Dusky Grasswren
Amytornis purnellii

At first glance the Dusky Grasswren looks more like a rat bounding over rocks with head down but tail high and quivering. The Dusky Grasswren is a cinnamon-brown grasswren with a thin bill. It has cinnamon-brown upperparts with long, pale streaks and rich-buff underparts. The flanks of the female are pale chestnut. Seeds, ants, beetles, grasshoppers, bugs and flies are picked from nooks. Flight is rare, the family

Dusky Grasswren
Amytornis purnellii

groups of birds relying on their legs to carry them to safety. If disturbed, they scatter in all directions. They call to regroup if they loose sight of each other, their call a silvery song 'scree-scree-scree teu teu'.

Striated Grasswren
Amytornis striatus

This is the only grass-wren south of the Tropic of Capricorn that is red-brown above and has a strong, black whisker-mark. Its head and back are marked with prominent white streaks and the underparts are buff-white. This is the most widespread of the grass-wrens. It is sedentary and bands together in loose groups. It forages by bounding along the ground with its tail cocked, looking for insects and seeds. It has a sweet, rippling song, interspersed with 'tu-tu-tu' notes.

Honeyeaters

Singing Honeyeater
Lichenostomus virescens

The Singing Honeyeater is Australia's most widespread honeyeater. It is a medium-sized, 17 to 22 cm, pale grey-brown honeyeater, with a bold black stripe from the bill through the eye and to the sides of the neck. There is a parallel yellow streak below, edged underneath with white and ending in a broad white mark. The underparts are off-white with slight, dark streaks. Belying its name,

its voice is a loud single, double or repeated 'prrp'. At dawn it voices a persistent 'kitch-ee-wok'. Singing Honeyeaters forage in shrubbery and low tree foliage. Their diet is eclectic: insects, nectar and fruit, even eggs from smaller birds are eaten, depending on what is available.

Spiny-cheeked Honeyeater
Acanthagenys rufogularis

The Spiny-cheeked Honeyeater is a large, 22 to 27 cm, graceful honeyeater, quite commonly seen, with a striking pink and black bill. It is generally brownish with a long tail and a strong dark mark through the eye over a broad, white streak along the cheek. The throat and upperbreast are pale pink to deep, sandy buff. The bird eats fruit as well as nectar and also insects. Spiny-cheeked Honeyeaters usually feed under cover, working quickly to the outside of foliage from within. Flight is a swift and undulating low dash to the next bush. During flight the white rump and tail tip contrast with the brown upperparts. The birds are noisy and individuals often break off from feeding by characteristically throwing their heads up in an unusual mixture of whistles, gurgles, trills and whines and the occasional explosive 'quock'. They can be found in pairs or in loose gatherings.

Yellow-throated Miner
Manorina flavigula

The Yellow-throated Miner is a 25 to 28 cm bird, with rump and whole undersurface whitish. The crown is grey and a black mark extends from the bill to under the eye and over the ear. The forehead and neck are washed yellow and there is an obvious patch of yellow skin behind the eye. Colonies of a dozen or so birds are seen. They have strong legs and sharp claws and use these to hang in bizarre postures. They hop about in the trees and bushes and on the ground looking for insects. They also take seeds and even nectar. They have a complex vocabulary of twitterings and squeaks and their commonest call is a querulous 'teee...teee... teeee'.

Grey-headed Honeyeater
Lichenostomus keart-landi

This unmistakable honeyeater, 15 to 17 cm, has a clear grey crown with slightly streaked lemon underparts. A black mask passes through the eye to the side of the head above a distinctive yellow plume. Grey-headed Honeyeaters occur in small, sedentary groups of five or six birds. They glean insects from branches and also sip nectar. Most feeding is done in the canopy, the groups chattering regularly through the day. Their calls vary from a loud 'kwot' to 'chee-toyt' to 'chek, chek, chek...'.

White-plumed Honeyeater *Licheno-stomus penicillatus*

One of the most widespread of honeyeaters, the White-plumed Honeyeater is 15 to 19 cm, plain olive-grey, with a yellow head, yellow

Singing Honeyeater
Lichenostomus virescens

wash on the wings and a long, white neck-plume, margined black above. The bird occurs in pairs or groups of up to 10. They feed from low to high in trees, gleaning insects and sipping nectar with their muscular tongue which is finely bristled at the tip. Nervously active, the birds bounce around in the foliage, turning this way and that and dashing from one tree to the next, one after the other, in twisting swoops or short glides with wings half open and held high.

Brown Honeyeater
Lichmera indistincta

The Brown Honeyeater is a 15 to 19 cm, plain, olive-brown honeyeater, with a longish, curved bill and a tiny yellowish and silvery-white spot behind the eye. This small, indistinct honeyeater has a rich and varied musical song. Brown Honeyeaters are opportunistic nectar-feeders. When there is no flowering the birds turn to insects, catching them among the foliage or in mid-air bursts from the high branches.

Spotted Bowerbird
Chlamydera maculata

These stocky, stout-billed birds are renowned for the bowers the males build for courting and mating. The Spotted Bowerbird is

Yellow-throated Miner
Manorina flavigula

a richly coloured, brown bird, 25 to 27 cm, blackish above and on the throat and upper breast. It has a prominent pattern of large golden-cream to rich buff spots, which becomes smaller on the throat and upper breast. Its lilac-pink crest is hidden except

BRUCE THOMSON

103

BRUCE THOMSON

Emu *Dromaius novaehollandiae*

during displays. It has an extraordinary variety of calls: penetrating chirring, grating and hissing noises; clinks; and mimics other noises. Mainly a fruit-eater, it picks drupes of mistle-toes within crowns of trees. In many areas this bird is limited to pockets of the Native Fig.

Emu *Dromaius novaehollandiae*

Perhaps Australia's most famous Big Bird. Up to almost 2 m tall, it must be

Southern Boobook *Ninox novaeseelandiae*

BRUCE THOMSON

104

an emu! The emu is herbivorous, feeding on fruits, seeds, flowers, insects and young growing parts of plants. They live in pairs from December to May, maintaining a large home range of tens of kilometres. The male then shepherds his tribe of up to (rarely) 20 chicks.

Nocturnal Birds

Barn Owl *Tyto alba*

Barn owls are 32 to 35 cm birds, that have flat, heart-shaped, white facial disks and dark eyes. They are pure-white below and usually seen at night flying in car headlights or sitting on a roadside fence. They can often be heard flying overhead uttering a rasping hiss. Their diet includes rodents, small marsupials, lizards and large insects.

Southern Boobook *Ninox novaeseelandiae*

The most abundant of Australian owls, the Southern Boobook is also called a 'mopoke', after its distinctive call. It is a small owl, 30 to 35 cm, with a hawk-like face. It appears to be wearing large, pale-rimmed goggles bordering the dark patch round each eye.

The underparts are reddish-brown, mottled with white. Boobooks eat birds up to the size of a small honeyeater and small mammals; they also eat invertebrates. They sit watchfully on exposed branches and feeding is done

in the first hour or two after dusk and then again before sunrise.

Spotted Nightjar *Caprimulgus guttatus*

The Spotted Nightjar is a small nocturnal bird, about 29 to 30 cm. It is the typical nightjar of the interior of Australia. It is a reddish-brown with a large, white window in its wing. By day the beautifully camouflaged bird roosts on bare ground. In the hours after sunset and before sunrise it hawks for insects with an erratic and jerky stiff-winged flight over treetops. Its voice is an eerie, accelerating 'caw-caw-cook-ook-ook', all on the same note.

Australian Owlet-nightjar *Aegotheles cristatus*

Australian Owlet-nightjar *Aegotheles cristatus*

The 22 cm Australian Owlet-nightjar is like a miniature owl. It is rusty-grey with large, black eyes and a double collar on its hindneck. It is a sedentary bird, keeping to the same patch of woodland year in, year out. If disturbed from its roosting site it will dash in an undulating flight directly to another hollow, revealing a great familiarity with its territory. The bird hunts for insects after dusk and before dawn, either hawking for them or adopting a perch-and-pounce strategy. It voice is a pleasant chuckle.

Spotted Nightjar
Caprimulgus guttatus

Spotted Nightjar

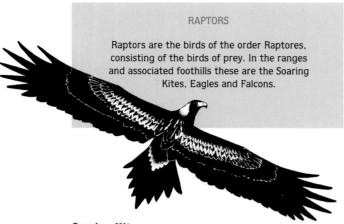

Soaring Kites

Black Kite
Milvus migrans

A long-winged, dark kite, about 52 cm long, with a wingspan of 1.2 m. It has a forked tail, which looks square in flight, constantly twisting and turning to stabilise the bird in flight. The plumage of this bird is a dark, muddy brown with fine, dark streaks. It has a dark mark around the eye and is paler on the throat. Its short legs are yellow. Black Kites are usually found in loose flocks of up to hundreds climbing the sky in slow, wheeling

Wedge-tailed Eagle
Aquila audax

companies. A fire or dead beast will attract them, as will rubbish dumps and slaughter yards. Its call is a feeble and plaintive whinny.

Whistling Kite
Haliastur sphenurus

This is a common and widespread kite which soars effortlessly. Its plumage is light brown with plentiful pale streaks on its head, back and breast. It has pale spots on its upperparts. The bird can be mistaken for the Black Kite but in flight the underwing pattern is distinctive with the pale forepart of the wing joining a cream band that crosses the wing near the tip, leaving a large, dark rectangle along the trailing edge. It does not flock in such great numbers as does the Black, nor manoeuvre its tail as much. Distinctive also is the shrill, whistling call; the first note leisurely, long and descending followed by a quick upward burst of four to six short, shrill staccato notes. The Whistling Kite feeds mainly on carrion.

Eagles

Wedge-tailed Eagle
Aquila audax

With a wingspan that can reach over 2.5 m this is the largest bird of prey in Australia. The Wedge-tailed Eagle is a huge, dark eagle with a pale bill, long, feathered legs and a long, diamond-shaped tail. It flies with easy, powerful wingbeats and soars to great heights in majestic circles, wings upswept. The bird will hunt live prey, especially rabbits, but it is mainly a carrion-eater with up to 30 birds congregating at a road-kill. The voice is a feeble 'pseet-you, pseet-you'.

Little Eagle
Hieraaetus morphnoides

Looking very much like a Whistling Kite, the Little Eagle can be distinguished by its stouter build, short, square tail and broader,

Wedge-tailed Eagle
Aquila audax

Nankeen Kestrel
Falco cenchroides

more rounded wings which are tipped up during flight. Its legs are feathered right to its toes and it has a little crest on its head. Birds occur in pairs and soar alone or together searching for live prey such as small mammals, reptiles, large insects and birds. The Little Eagle will eat carrion. Its voice is a loud rapid 'who-whee-whit'; also a penetrating 'kuk-kuk-kuk'.

Whistling Kite
*Haliastur
sphenurus*

Falcons

Brown Falcon
Falco berigora

This 50 cm long bird has a wingspan of less than a metre. It is one of the most widespread and abundant raptors. Its plumage is variable and it can be mistaken for a number of other raptors. Two features, however, are constant: a double moustache mark enclosing a paler cheek-patch; and buff to pale red-brown notching of flight and tail feathers. In flight its wings are held up in a V-shape. The Brown Falcon's main method of searching for food is to sit quietly on a high perch, dropping down on victims. Usually seen alone or in pairs, it is the noisiest of Australian raptors with screeches and a demented, hoarse cackling.

Nankeen Kestrel
Falco cenchroides

The Nankeen Kestrel is a small falcon, about 30 cm, with a wingspan of 75 cm. It hunts in a distinctive manner, hovering—almost

hanging—in mid-air at one spot for minutes at a time, watching the ground with wings quivering and tail fanned. When it sees prey it drops in steps and then plummets head first onto the victim. It has pale rufous upperparts with contrasting black flight feathers and whitish underparts. The voice is shrill rapid-fire 'kikikikikiki'.

Little Eagle
Hieraaetus morphnoides

107

Reptiles

While the desert ranges, with their reliable supplies of nutrition and water are the domain of birds and mammals, reptiles are nevertheless a common sight. Below are examples of lizards that you will most likely see. While some require a specific rocky habitat most will also occur in the adjacent broad-sweep landscapes where lizards come into their own. Not surprisingly you will more likely see snakes in the ranges than in the surrounding habitats because they prefer a richer diet of birds, lizards and mammals.

Goannas
(monitor lizards)

Perentie
Varanus giganteus

The Perentie is Australia's largest lizard and second

DIURNAL REPTILES—those active by day—in the desert ranges and associated foothills include the goannas, dragons and skinks. The only NOCTURNAL REPTILE in this habitat—besides the snakes which are mostly nocturnal—is a Gecko.

largest in the world after the Komodo Dragon of Indonesia. Growing up to 2 m in length, the Perentie is a rich brown above, its back and sides sprinkled with creamy-yellow blotches, edged black. On the neck the blotches join to form a distinctive reticulated pattern, like paving done with hexagonal-shaped blocks. This ground-dwelling lizard inhabits deep crevices in rocky outcrops but is found also in the adjacent sandy desert. It feeds on carrion and living prey including other lizards.

Varanus tristis

Growing to a total length of about 80 cm this goanna

is normally a tree-dweller, but also inhabits rocky crevices in Central Australia. It is brown to black with many small, pale spots, each with a dark centre. It has a distinctive black tail. Its diet is similar to that of the Perentie.

Dragons

Ring-tailed Dragon
Ctenophorus caudicinctus

A swift dragon, about 20 cm full length, the Ring-tailed Dragon is found living amongst rocks where it forages for insects. It is orange-brown above and has dark brown or black rings along its tail. The tail

Perentie *Varanus giganteus*

Cryptoblepharus plagiocephalus

Varanus tristis

is up to twice as long as the body. It often dashes long distances, at great speed, for cover.

Skinks

Cryptoblepharus plagiocephalus

A small, about 10 cm long, active, diurnal lizard which feeds on insects. It is grey, with a vague ragged-edged pale stripe from above the eye to the tail. The stripe is bordered by dark blotches. The limbs are also flecked with brown and white. It is a tree-dwelling lizard that

can also be found around buildings.

Firetail Skink
Morethia ruficauda

As the name suggests this lizard is distinguished by its bright red tail. Its dark body has two distinct white stripes. This lizard forages for insects amongst rocky outcrops particularly where vegetation is richest, in gullies or near creeks or water-holes. It is about 7 cm long.

Ring-tailed Dragon
Ctenophorus caudicinctus

Geckos

Marbled Velvet Gecko
Oedura marmorata

Soft-bodied nocturnal lizards, geckos use their fleshy tongues to keep their lidless eyes clean. The Marbled Velvet Gecko is a variable gecko but is typically a yellow-banded, purplish-brown lizard. It is about 14 cm long and more-or-less confined to stony areas in Central Australia.

109

Firetail Skink
Morethia ruficauda

head, narrow neck, short stout body and thin rat-like tail ending in a curved, soft spine. Its colour is reddish-brown. During the day they are found half-buried in sand, soil and litter, usually under a shrub or tree. They attract prey—mammals and reptiles—by twitching the tip of the tail as a lure.

Stimson's Python
Liasis stimsoni

NON-VENOMOUS. Pythons are slow-moving snakes which feed largely on birds and mammals. Mostly nocturnal, they can be found basking through the day. Stimson's Python is typically reddish-brown above, but paler on the lower sides. It often does not have a distinct pattern but sometimes has a series of

King Brown Snake
Pseudechis australis

Marbled Velvet Gecko
Oedura marmorata

Snakes

King Brown Snake
Pseudechis australis

DANGEROUS. A rich copper-coloured to dark olive-brown snake, with a cream belly often scattered with orange blotches. The individual scales give the overall impression of a reticulated pattern. The snake is 2 m long, widespread and is nocturnal in the hotter parts of its territory. It feeds on mammals, reptiles and frogs and is found in a wide range of habitats.

Desert Death Adder
Acanthophis pyrrhus

DANGEROUS. A viper-like snake characterised by a broad, somewhat triangular

irregular, darker blotches along the back and sides. The head is a uniform light brown or with blotches. There is a dark streak through each eye and lips are pale. A small python, it grows to about 1 m. It feeds on reptiles, mammals and birds and can be found in caves, rock crevices and even in trees.

Desert Death Adder
Acanthophis pyrrhus

Stimson's Python
Liasis stimsoni

BRUCE THOMSON

111

Black-footed Rock-wallaby
Petrogale lateralis

rock outcrops with deep cracks and caves with nearby feeding areas of grass and herbs at the base, on top, or along terraces. Simpsons Gap and Redbank Gorge are two such places, but there are many more in the ranges.

Bats

In Australia's arid zone bats are most abundant in the resource-rich areas such as the desert ranges where they inhabit caves or rocky crannies. They also roost in large trees along the rivers spilling from the ranges.

Mammals

Marsupials

Euro *Macropus robustus*

From head to tail the Euro is about 1.5 to 2 m. The female is smaller (about 25 kg) than the male (about 45 kg). This dark grey to reddish, stocky kangaroo has shaggy fur and lives in the rocky ranges where caves and overhangs provide shelter. An essentially solitary animal, it grazes in the cool of the evening on grasses and shrubs within a limited home range which may include the surrounding plains.

Black-footed Rock-wallaby *Petrogale lateralis*

This pretty little rock wallaby is restricted to the Central Australian Ranges. It is about 1 m long from nose to tail and weighs

around 4 kg. It is reddish-brown above which grades to grey on the neck and shoulders. It has a pale cheek-stripe, underlined by a dark brown stripe, as well as a white side-stripe underlined with a dark brown stripe. The tail grades to black towards the tip. As the name suggests, rock-wallabies live in rocky habitats. Their optimum habitat includes extensive

Little Mastiff-bat
Mormopterus planiceps

Little Mastiff-bat *Mormopterus planiceps*

A common species, it is usually found in association with the open woodlands and riverine environments at the flanks of the ranges. The Little Mastiff-bat flies in open and unobstructed environments. This small

Little Mastiff-bat
Mormopterus planiceps

Gould's Wattled Bat
Chalinolobus gouldii

bat, body size 5 to 7 cm and tail 2 to 3 cm, is light brown to light greyish-brown. The base of the hair is lighter than the tips. The bare skin regions are pink or pigmented light grey.

Lesser Long-eared Bat
Nyctophilus geoffroyi

A common species, this bat prefers woodlands and tree-lined water-courses though it can be found in caves and rock crevices and even in the folds of hessian bags, old coats and other material left hanging about on verandahs and in sheds. Typically, this bat flies at a height of 6 to 9 m, diving suddenly to intercept insects below. This small bat—body size 4 to 5 cm and tail about 3 to 4 cm—is brownish-grey above and pale grey below. The base of the hair is darker than the tips. The bare regions of the skin are lightly pigmented greyish-pink.

Lesser Long-eared Bat *Nyctophilus geoffroyi*

Gould's Wattled Bat
Chalinolobus gouldii

A widely distributed bat, Gould's Wattled Bat is found in woodlands and open forests where it hunts for insects well above tree height. A small bat—body size 6 to 7 cm and tail 3 to 5 cm—it is dark brown above with hair on the head and shoulders often black. Below it is mid- to dark brown. Bare skin is pigmented mid- to dark brownish-grey.

Meat ant *Iridomyrmex* sp.

Arthropods

Ants

Like plants and other animals, ants have distinguishing characteristics which can be used as a guide to their identification. Myrmecologists (scientists who study ants) use a variety of features to describe ants, for example, the placement of ants' antennae, the size and shape of

Golden Spiny Ant
Polyrhachis sp.

their waist segment, or petiole, the presence of spines and the general sculpted shape.

Golden Spiny Ant
Polyrhachis sp.

The Golden Spiny Ant has a distinctive golden gaster, imparted by golden hairs, and spectacular-looking spines. This ant is ancestrally a tropical ant and probably prefers rocky habitat because its more constant productivity closely resembles the productivity of the tropics.

Black Meat Ant
Iridomyrmex viridiaeneus

The common Black Meat Ant of Central Australia is well adapted to arid conditions. It is found in numbers swarming over bare patches of ground.

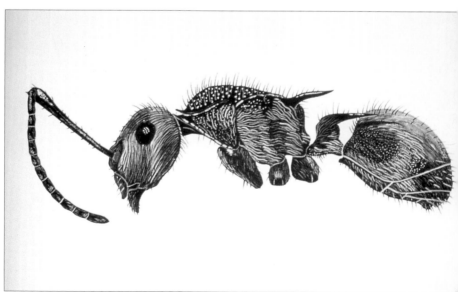

ILLUSTRATION BY PETER JACKLYN

Permanent waterhole on Finke River at Glen Helen Gorge in the Western MacDonnells.

CHAPTER SIX

Riverine Woodlands

Introduction

The desert rivers, such as the Finke River, spilling out of the ranges are themselves ribbons of refuge habitat. The permanent watertable, small gullies and water-holes along their length, provide a reliable habitat for birds, fish and plants. Trees, such as the River Red Gum, along with pockets of Coolibahs on the clayey soils, line the watercourses right across the arid zone of Australia. These trees are analogous to a multi-storey, high density housing development for birds, particularly parrots. The rich understorey of the riverine woodlands contains perennial grasses which are dependent on a regular water supply. It is also here that many of the introduced plants of Central Australia have taken a foothold.

A surprise to most visitors, is that our rivers rarely run with water. These rivers of sand spill out and onto the desert plains surrounding the ranges where the water evaporates. These 'flood-outs' are themselves rich habitat and a stronghold for the cattle industry. The Finke River, the largest in Central Australia, floods-out into the Simpson Desert, rarely, if ever, reaching Lake Eyre.

PLANTS OF THE RIVERINE WOODLANDS

Upper-storey plants

See page 74 for a brief description of the genus *Acacia*.

Acacia estrophiolata
(Ironwood)

This graceful tree grows to 15 m and has pendulous or

Acacia georginae
(Gidgee)

This spreading, often straggly tree grows to 5 m. It is often multi-trunked. The tree has a dense crown and offers deep shade. The phyllodes are narrow and tapered toward both ends, 4 to 11 cm x 0.4 to 1.6 cm. The globular flower-head has 12 to 25 flowers. The

a shrub or tree growing to 5 m high. The branches have a whitish, waxy covering. The leaves are long, flat and narrow, 5 to 18 cm x 0.2 to 1 cm, with a central vein. The globular flower-heads are deep golden and contain 25 to 50 flowers. The heads are in clusters. The light brown, papery pods, 8 cm x 1 cm, are flat and raised over the seeds.

Acacia estrophiolata
(Ironwood)

Acacia georginae (Gidgee)

weeping branchlets, though young trees have a strict erect habit. The flat, pale green leaves are narrow, 4 to 11 cm x 0.2 to 0.4 cm. The flower-heads comprise about 30 flowers and are pale yellow and globular-shaped. The narrow pods are constricted between the seeds. The wood is very hard, hence the common name.

pods are curved, 6 to 13 cm x 1.2 to 2.5 cm. In humid or rainy weather the tree can give off an unpleasant smell, rather like cat's urine.

Acacia murrayana
(Colony Wattle)

Colony Wattle, as the name suggests, grows extensively in colonies. Colony Wattle is

Acacia murrayana (Colony Wattle)

Acacia georginae (Gidgee)

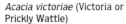

Acacia murrayana (Colony Wattle)

Acacia victoriae
(Victoria or Prickly
Wattle)

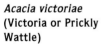
Acacia victoriae (Victoria or Prickly Wattle)

This shrub or straggly tree grows up to 8 m tall, often forming thickets. Many of the trees have prickles. Young branches are green. The leaves have a central vein and are flat, narrow and pointed, 1.5 to 8.5 cm x 0.2 to 1 cm. The flower-heads are pale yellow and have 22 to 34 flowers. The light brown, papery pods, 9 cm x 2 cm, are flat though raised over the seed. Thickets of *A. victoriae* are obvious on the alluvial sand-plains surrounding Alice Springs in good years.

117

See page 81 for a brief description of the genus *Eucalyptus*.

Eucalyptus camaldulensis (River Red Gum)

This magnificent tree, growing up to 45 m, but commonly 26 to 36 m tall, is the most widespread Eucalypt in Australia. The bark is smooth, white and often with grey or red patches. The bark flakes off in summer. The adult leaves are alternate, narrow, 6 to 30 cm x 1 to 2 cm and pale green in colour (sometimes grey-

Eucalyptus camaldulensis (River Red Gum)

green). The globular buds, 0.6 to 1.2 cm x 0.3 to 0.5 cm, occur in clusters of seven to eleven and have pointed caps. Flowers are cream. The fruit or gumnut has valves protruding.

Eucalyptus papuana (Ghost Gum)

The Ghost Gum is one of the Centre's most distinctive Eucalypts, its beautiful white trunk almost shimmering against the red rock on which it often grows. The

Eucalyptus papuana
(Ghost Gum)

Eucalyptus coolibah ssp. *arida* (Coolibah)

Ghost Gum is a tree, 5 to 15 m high, but sometimes growing to 20 m. Its adult long, narrow leaves, 5 to 18 cm x 1.2 to 4.5 cm, hang down in clusters on drooping branchlets. The buds are in clusters of five to eleven, developing into cream flowers. The gumnuts are small and cylindrical, 0.7 to 1 cm x 0.6 to 0.9 cm, with valves inside.

Eucalyptus coolibah ssp. *arida* (Coolibah)

This is the famous tree of Australian folklore. It grows to 22 m and becomes gnarled with age. Bark is usually rough, dark grey on the trunk and larger branches, while upper branches are often smooth white or grey. The grey-green, tapered leaves are three times as long as

'Once a jolly swagman camped by a billabong, under the shade of a Coolibah tree'

WALTZING MATILDA
BANJO PATERSON

wide, 7 to 15 cm x 1.8 to 3 cm. The oval buds, which occur in clusters of three to seven, erupt into white or cream flowers. The fruits are small, only 0.2 to 0.3 cm.

Eucalyptus coolibah ssp. *arida* (Coolibah)

Melaleuca glomerata
(Inland Teatree)

Teatrees *Melaleuca glomerata* (left) and *M. linariifolia* (right)

high. The young branchlets and leaves are covered with hair which makes the plant look silvery under a Central sunny sky. The leaves are narrow and pointed, 1 to 5 cm long. The flowers are crowded into a globular, creamy flower-head with pale yellow stamens and form tiny, closely packed, globular gumnuts, about 0.2 cm.

Melaleuca glomerata (Inland Teatree)

Inland Teatree belongs to the Myrtaceae family, the same family as Eucalypts. Like Eucalypts, the Melaleuca flowers grow in cups which develop into a woody fruit like a gumnut. Melaleucas are also commonly known as paperbarks because it is possible to pull the bark off in wide strips. Inland Teatree grows as a spreading shrub up to 3 m

Muehlenbeckia florulenta (Lignum)

Lignum belongs to the family Polygonaceae. Lignum is a much-stemmed, intricately branching shrub, 2 to 4 m high. The leaves are rarely present since they drop as the plant matures. The small, almost insignificant flowers grow in clusters. The fruit is a shiny nut 0.5 cm long. Lignum grows in swampy areas.

Ground-storey plants

Atriplex nummularia (Old Man Saltbush)

Old Man Saltbush belongs to the Chenopodiaceae or saltbush family. The family is important in the southern part of arid Australia since it forms a staple for the vast cattle and

Chenopodium auricomum
(Bluebush)

sheep stations. Old Man Saltbush is probably the best known saltbush in Central Australia. It is a large, blue-grey bush, 2 to 3 m high, with a mealy or scaly covering. The leaves are on stalks and are

Atriplex nummularia
(Old Man Saltbush)

Chenopodium auricomum
(Bluebush)

almost circular, about 2 cm long. Male and female flowers are on separate bushes. The flowers are small and without any petals in the usual sense. After fertilisation, the leafy bracts of the female flower develop into a fan-shaped fruit.

Muehlenbeckia florulenta
(Lignum)

Chenopodium auricomum (Bluebush)

The Bluebush belongs to the Chenopodiaceae, or saltbush, family. The plant takes its common name from the grey, mealy covering on the leaves that make the bush look blue. Leaves are alternate and elliptical in shape, 2 to 5 cm long. Flowers are pale yellow on a branching spike, about 10 cm long.

121

ANIMALS OF THE RIVERINE
WOODLANDS

The riverine woodlands are corridors of refuge habitat. Together with the tree-hollows provided by River Red Gums and Coolibahs, the riverine habitat provides a reliable source of food. This habitat has a large population of resident birds.

Birds

Parrots and Cockatoos

Budgerigar
Melopsittacus undulatus

Perhaps the world's best known parrot, with as much variety in colour as flavours in ice-cream. The wild, 'true-blue' population, however, has only one plumage—mainly yellow and green.

Budgerigar
Melopsittacus undulatus

Growing up to 20 cm, the Budgerigar has a yellow forehead and throat with close, dark barrings. In flight it flashes almost iridescent yellows and greens when the sun strikes. Budgerigars are highly nomadic, following flushes of seeding grass after storms. Budgies live in flocks of 100 or so birds and activities occur as a flock. Their voice is a musical, mellow chirrup and sharp, rasping scolds.

Cockatiel
Nymphicus hollandicus

The Cockatiel is the only smallish, 32 cm, Australian parrot with a crest. It has largely grey plumage set off by prominent white shoulders. The central tail feathers are long and slender. The male has a yellow face with an orange ear patch and his

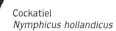

Cockatiel
Nymphicus hollandicus

tail is plain. The female's face is paler and her tail and abdomen are barred. Cockatiels gather in groups of five to very large flocks. They are seed-eaters and forage mainly on the ground. Their flight, easy, graceful and buoyant on

Galah *Cacatua roseicapilla*

steadily beating wings with swept wings and tail, is conspicuous. Their contact call is a prolonged, warbling 'queel-queel' repeated three or four times, followed by a brief pause and then repeated.

Galah
Cacatua roseicapilla

The Galah is one of Australia's most loved and most beautiful birds. A small pink and grey cockatoo, about 36 cm, it is pale grey above, rose-pink to deep rose-red below, with low cap-like crest. This bird is usually seen in flocks of 30 to 1000. The flight of the Galah, much loved by cartoonists, is a continuous, deep flapping, swaying from side to side (like a silly galah!). It is a seed-eater and its call is a single-note screech in contact with harsh screeching at other times.

Little Corella
Cacatua sanguinea

Little Corella
Cacatua sanguinea

A smallish, white cockatoo, about 38 cm long, including its round tail. It has a short, whitish bill, a pink stain between bill and eye and a bare, blue-grey

Pink Cockatoo
Cacatua leadbeateri

eyepatch. The Little Corella is found in pairs to enormous, noisy flocks. They eat on the ground, feeding on seeds of grasses and legumes. The flight is swift, direct and pigeon-like and the wings are slender. It has more than 10 calls, the most common is an unforgettable raucous screech.

Pink Cockatoo
Cacatua leadbeateri

A beautiful, sunset pink-washed, white cockatoo, about 36 cm. It has an

Ringneck Parrot
Barnadius zonarius

seed and particularly like the seeds of acacias and the cypress pine. To keep contact they voice a peculiar quavering 'quee..er', or otherwise harsh screeches.

Red-tailed Black Cockatoo *Calyptorhynchus magnificus*

A large, black cockatoo up to 66 cm. It is the only large black cockatoo in the Centre and is conspicuous and noisy. The male is black all over excepting the broad, scarlet panels in the tail which are conspicuous in take off and landing. The female is black with yellow spots and yellow bars on her underparts. Her tail panels are yellow-orange. The Red-tailed Black Cockatoo flies with slow, funereal wing-beats, almost rowing through the sky. They are found in pairs, family groups or small parties, feeding high in the trees on seeds and more rarely on the ground. Their voice is a far-carrying bugle or trumpet, 'kreee', screeched in flight at regular intervals or when perched in the tree.

Ringneck Parrot *Barnadius zonarius*

A distinctive and robust parrot, 34 to 38 cm. The only green Australian parrot with a blackish head. It has a long tail, a yellow ring on

its hindneck and a yellow zone across its breast. Ringnecks are seen in ones and twos or in small family groups. They feed on the seeds of grasses and herbs, eucalypts, cypress pines and acacias, fruit blossoms, leaf buds and occasionally even insects and their larvae. Never moving far from their birth place, they are nevertheless strong fliers, vigorously flapping low amongst trees and then gliding with their wings folded, swooping onto a branch to land

Sacred Kingfisher
Halcyon sancta

with tail fanned. On the wing they have a strident contact call 'kwink...kwink... kwink...'. In alarm they have a rapid harsh chattering 'chuk, chuk, chuk'.

Pied Butcherbird *Cracticus nigrogularis*

A conspicuous, 35 cm, black and white bird, with a pure and glorious voice. The white body is set off by a

upswept crest which is whitish when folded and when spread shows bands of scarlet and yellow. Distinctive in flight, it has quick, shallow and irregular wing-beats interspersed with glides on downswept wings. It is usually found in pairs and small groups, sometimes in the company of Galahs or Little Corellas. Pink Cockatoos spend most of the day feeding on the ground or among branches of trees and shrubs. They eats nuts, fruits, roots and

Pied Butcherbird
Cracticus nigrogularis

Black-breasted Kite
Hamirostra melanosternon

wholly black head, throat and upperbreast. The wings and back are black, except for a conspicuous white panel on the wings. The straight bill is finely hooked at the tip. Singly or in pairs, the birds hunt by perch-and-pounce, picking off insects, reptiles, small mammals and even other birds. They fly swiftly from point-to-point and swoop up to a new perch. Their voice is a slow flute-like piping—one of the purest sounds of the Australian bush.

Sacred Kingfisher
Halcyon sancta

A small kingfisher, 19 to 23 cm. The male Sacred King-fisher has blue shoulders, a bright blue rump and bright, deep blue tail. Collar and underparts are white.

The female is larger, duller and greener. The Sacred Kingfisher is a land king-fisher and is usually solitary. The diet is mainly small reptiles, crickets, grasshoppers, beetles and their larvae. It spends much of its time sitting very quiet-ly on a low branch looking down for prey which the birds plunge onto. The voice is a distinctive descending 'kik-kik-kik-kik-kik'.

Black-breasted Kite
Hamirostra melanoster-non

Otherwise known as the Black-Breasted Buzzard, this bird is about 60 cm long and has a wingspan of 1.5 m. It is usually seen soaring high with large wings upswept and back-swept. The wings have a distinctive, round, white window near the black wingtips. The short, rounded, buff tail is also distinctive. This solitary bird is an inveterate nest robber, feeding the snatched young to its own chicks. Its main food includes reptiles, grasshop-pers, many birds and mammals. Its voice is a short, hoarse yelp.

Reptiles

As well as those described below, all the reptiles of the desert ranges (see page 108) can also be found in the riverine habitat.

Tree Dtella
Gehyra variegata

This is a highly variable gecko, about 12 cm long. It is grey or purplish-grey above with irregular black-ish marbling. A tree-dwelling lizard, during the day it will hide under loose bark.

Spiny-tailed Gecko
Diplodactylus ciliarus

The Spiny-tailed Gecko is another highly variable gecko, also about 12 cm long. In the Centre it is likely to be reddish-brown with a broad, mottled pat-tern made up of groups of grey, orange or white scales. The colour and pat-tern of the iris is striking

Tree Dtella
Gehyra variegata

and complex. This is normally a tree-dwelling lizard, though it can be found amongst spinifex where there are few trees.

also among rocks. It has two cream or yellow strips running down its back from the nape of the neck to the base of

Spiny-tailed Gecko
Diplodactylus ciliarus

Snakes

Central Australian Diamond Python
Morelia bredli

NON-VENOMOUS. A beautiful, strickingly patterned python of contrasting pale, dark-edged spots, blotches, bands and stripes. Generally brownish or reddish-brown above, with a white, cream or yellow belly, variegated with dark brown or grey. The average length is about 2 m. The lips are paler and barred with dark brown, the top lip with shallow pits. The under-surface is white or creamy-yellow. This can be a tree-dwelling python.

Stimson's Python
Liasis stimsoni

NON-VENOMOUS. The average length of this python is only about 1 m. It is rich light brown above, paler lower on the sides. It has a strongly contrasting pat-

Central Australian Diamond Python
Morelia bredli

Lophognathus longirostris

A slender, tree-dwelling, reddish-brown lizard, found along watercourses, but

the tail. The back of the neck has a row of spine-like scales and there is a white or cream stripe along the lower jaw. The total length of the lizard is about 18 cm.

BRUCE THOMSON

Stimson's Python
Liasis stimsoni

tern of irregular, darker brown blotches, often elongated into bands. There is a dark streak through each

eye. It is found in a wide variety of arid environments but is often associated with larger trees like those of the dry watercourses.

Lophognathus longirostris

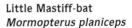
Mammals

Bats

Little Mastiff-bat
Mormopterus planiceps

A common species, it is usually found in association with the open woodlands and riverine environments at the flanks of the ranges. The Little Mastiff-bat flies in open and unobstructed environments. This small bat, body size 5 to 7 cm and tail 2 to 3 cm, is light brown to light greyish-brown. The base of the hair is lighter than the tips. The bare skin regions are pink or pigmented light grey.

Little Mastiff-bat
*Mormopterus
planiceps*

Lesser Long-eared Bat *Nyctophilus geoffroyi*

A common species, this bat prefers woodlands and tree-lined watercourses though it can be found in caves and rock crevices and even in the folds of hessian bags, old coats and other material left hanging about on verandahs and in sheds. Typically, this bat flies at a height of 6 to 9 m, diving suddenly to intercept insects below. This small bat—body size 4 to 5 cm and tail about 3 to 4 cm—is brownish-grey above and pale grey below. The base of the hair is darker than the tips. The bare regions of the skin are lightly pigmented greyish-pink.

Arthropods

Desert Bull-dog Ant *Myrmecia desertorum*

This is the only large bull-dog species found in Central Australia. It occurs in all mainland states. All but one of the greater than 100 species of *Myrmecia* occur in Australia. The Desert Bull-dog Ant usually exceeds 8 mm in length. Its eyes are large and its mandibles are long, slender and toothed.

Bull-dog Ant
Myrmecia sp.

CHAPTER SEVEN

Mulga Woodlands

Introduction

Mulga woodland grows mainly on red earths; essentially the unfertile detritus of weathered rock washed over millennia from the worn ranges, hills and tablelands onto the surrounding, almost imperceptible slopes and earth-curved plains.

It is an Australian paradox that in this infertile environment where at best you might expect a few tufts of wire grass, grow the highest densities of woody shrubs on the continent. By extracting nutrients deep in the soil and recycling them in leaf fall, individual plants act as nutrient pumps. The mulga roots are aided by nodular factories of symbiotic bacteria which convert atmospheric nitrogen (an essential nutrient) into a form accessible to the roots. Productivity can be measured in terms of leaf fall, which can vary from 40 kg/ha to 6000 kg/ha after a series of wet years.

And all this in one of the most unpredictable climates in the world; a characteristic of the mulga lands is the unreliability, in amount and season, of rainfall. In fact, mulga is conspicuously absent from semi-arid regions where there is a regular summer or winter drought.

Because mulga trees effectively use their shape to channel water down to their trunks and into the ground (see the *Acacia aneura* description below) they

act as mini-refuges for plants such as grasses and herbs, even ferns, which can survive in these small, favourable pockets during drought and, when conditions improve, recolonise the drier zones ensuring the survival of the community as a whole.

By using such a strategy these perennial plants avoid the direct impact of extremes. Much of the wildlife of the mulga (and the arid zone in general) use similar tactics. They burrow, work night-shift or generally forage at the least stressful time. The strategy is so successful that water becomes a secondary issue. For the desert-dwellers, food and water often occurs in one packet so that it is food that is most critical. Food is, in turn, influenced by the availability of nutrients in the system; so that the effect of the barren soils on which mulga ekes out a living cascades down to the very foundation of food webs dependent on mulga.

Social insects such as ants and termites are particularly abundant in the mulga-land's infertile and uncertain environment. This dominance by invertebrates anchors the food web which can then ramify into a network of other invertebrate and vertebrate predators including the Barking Spider, carnivorous marsupials and a host of lizards. Not surprisingly, there is also an abundance of insectivorous birds in the mulga woodlands.

MULGA
(*Acacia aneura*)

Australia, where rainfall is extremely unpredictable, the mulga phyllodes are actually longer and narrower than those of mulga trees elsewhere in the arid zone, effectively extending the catchment.

Stemflow waters infiltrate the ground within 45 cm of large tree trunks and within 15 cm of stems of small trees. Incredibly,

ite. The different abilities to cope with fire between spinifex grasslands and mulga woodlands often results in sharp boundaries separating these communities.

In the outback, the word 'mulga' is often used in a general way to lump together any large, perennial, woody *Acacia* species. This reflects the incred-

Mulga is highly resistant to moisture stress. The phyllodes (leaves) are vertically aligned to reduce heat load (the same principle explains why a person's legs do not get as sunburnt as their shoulders which are horizontally displayed) and this together with high oil content, sunken stomates, abundant leaf hairs and reduced leaf size, act to reduce transpiration losses. The colour of the foliage, a silvery blue-green, also acts to increase leaf reflectance.

Most ingenious, however, is the fact that individual mulga trees form their own catchment (though the concept also applies to other desert-dwelling trees). The common mulga shape is like an umbrella blown inside-out. This shape is most efficient at intercepting rain and allows mulga to channel what rainfall is available, down their phyllodes and stems, so that it concentrates at the base of the trunk where roots proliferate. Mulga phyllodes are long and narrow and directed upwards, enhancing the channelling of water. Here in Central

from a rainfall of only 25 mm, the equivalent of 140 mm of rain can enter the soil in this zone. Water from even small showers can be utilised more readily by mulga for a longer period than, say, the grass and shrub species in the same environment because the water is stored at a greater depth close to the tree.

While mulga can easily cope with the capriciousness of rain in the arid zone, it does not tolerate frequent fire. It has some resprouting ability from the roots but none from the stems. In fact, even if only the canopy has been burned the tree will die in a few years. While germination from seed is enhanced after fire, it is not a prerequis-

ible amount of variation in phyllode type and habit within Mulga (*Acacia aneura*) itself—it is even common practice to enter *A. aneura* several times in identification keys. Mulga phyllode width, for instance, varies from 0.1 cm to 1.2 cm; its length from 1 cm to 25 cm; and the foliage colour from green to grey and silvery blue. The pods, or legumes, also vary from 1.5 cm to 7 .5 cm in length and 0.4 cm to 1.5 cm in width. They can be paper thin to leathery or even woody.

There are almost certainly several species in the knot of genetically labile and currently evolving taxa we call *Acacia aneura* but as yet they have not been teased out by botanists.

PLANTS OF THE MULGA WOODLANDS

Most of the commonly seen plants associated with mulga woodlands are also found in the ranges and foothills.

Upper-storey plants

See page 74 for a brief description of the genus *Acacia*.

Acacia estrophiolata (Ironwood)

This graceful tree grows to 15 m and has pendulous or weeping branchlets, though young trees have a strict erect habit. The flat, pale green leaves are narrow, 4 to 11 cm x 0.2 to 0.4 cm. The flower-heads comprise about 30 flowers and are pale yellow and globular-shaped. The narrow pods are constricted between the seeds. The wood is very hard, hence the common name.

Acacia kempeana (Witchetty Bush)

Commonly known as Witchetty Bush because Aboriginal people eat witchetty grubs from the

Acacia estrophiolata
(Ironwood)

roots, *A. kempeana* grows as a spreading shrub or tree up to 5 m tall. The grey-green phyllodes are narrow and elliptical, 3 to 7.5 cm x 0.4 to 1.5 cm and have rounded ends. The flower-heads are golden spikes about 1 to 2 cm long. The papery pods are flat, about 5 cm x 1 cm.

Acacia kempeana
(Witchetty Bush)

Acacia tetragono-phylla (Dead Finish)

Dead Finish is the common name for this plant because by the time cattle resort to eating its sharp foliage, conditions are just about as bad as they can get—the dead finish. Dead Finish is a straggly bush growing up to 5 m high. Its

Acacia kempeana
(Witchetty Bush)

Acacia tetragonophylla
(Dead Finish)

Atalaya hemiglauca (Whitewood)

Whitewood belongs to the Sapindaceae family. The smooth, whitish-grey tree grows to 5 m. The divided leaves have 2 to 6 pairs of long, narrow, leathery leaflets, 6 to 20 cm x 0.8 to 2 cm, which hang down. The bell-shaped, white flowers hang in large clusters. The white, silky petals are oval-shaped, about 0.8 cm x 0.4 cm in size. The hairy fruit consists of two or three winged fruitlets joined together. Each fruitlet is 3 to 4 cm long including the wing.

four-sided, needle-like phyllodes, 1 to 6 cm x 0.1 cm, end in needle-sharp points. The golden, globular flowerhead is densely packed with around 50 flowers. The pods are narrow and twisted and up to 13 cm long. The seeds are surrounded by yellow arils which attract birds and large-bodied ants.

Acacia tetragonophylla
(Dead Finish)

Atalaya hemiglauca
(Whitewood)

Capparis mitchellii
(Wild Orange)

The Wild Orange belongs to the Capparaceae, or caper, family. Wild Orange develops from a prickly, much-branched shrub into a small tree. As a tree it has a dense canopy which makes it look a little like an orange tree, hence the common name. The undersides of the oval, leathery leaves, 3 to 6.5 cm long, are like grey felt due to their hairy covering. The large, pale yellow flowers grow in groups of

Capparis mitchellii
(Wild Orange)

Capparis spinosa
(Wild Passionfruit)

134

Enchylaena tomentosa
(Ruby Saltbush)

one to four on the end of twigs where each flower grows on its own stem and has fringed petals about 3 cm long. About 120 stamens spray from the flower. The fruit, which grows in the centre of the flower, is globular and hairy and smells strongly when ripe. The flesh between the seeds is edible.

Enchylaena tomentosa
(Ruby Saltbush)

Ruby Saltbush, as the name suggests, belongs to the Chenopodiaceae, or saltbush, family. Ruby Saltbush is a straggling, small shrub which grows to 1 m high. Its slender leaves are succulent, 0.8 to 2 cm long and covered with fine, downy hair which extends to the stems. The tiny flowers are hard to see but the fleshy, red, 0.5 cm wide fruits or berries make this plant easy to identify. The fleshy parts of the fruits are edible.

Eremophila freelingii
(Rock Fuchsia)

See page 80 for a brief description of the genus Eremophilla.

Often looking more dead than alive, these 1 to 2 m high bushes have hairy, greyish, narrow, aromatic leaves, 3 to 8 cm x 0.3 to 1 cm, which can often be waxy. The tubular flower has flaring lobes. The flower is usually lilac but can be pink, blue or even white. The ovoid, 0.6 to 0.8 cm long fruit is glandular and hairy.

Eremophila freelingii
(Rock Fuchsia)

Eremophila latrobei
(Latrobe's Desert Fuchsia)

This 1 to 3 m high bush is most easily recognised in flower when it is covered with bright red blooms. The leaves vary from narrow, green and almost hairless, to wider, hairy and grey-green, 1 to 8 cm x 0.5 to 5 cm. The conical fruit is 5 to 10 cm long.

Eremophila longifolia
(Weeping Emu Bush)

This shrub to small tree, 1 to 6 m high, has weeping branches. The dull green leaves are narrow and up to 15 cm long, normally sparsely haired. One to three brick red, spotted flowers grow out of the leaf axils. There is an obvious knob at the base of the flowers. The fleshy fruit becomes purple when ripe and is a favoured food of Emus.

Eremophila freelingii (Rock Fuchsia)

Eremophila latrobei
(Latrobe's Desert Fuchsia)

seven, developing into cream flowers. The large, pink-stalked gumnuts are oval-shaped—almost urn-like—2 to 2.5 cm wide, with the valves inside.

Hakea suberea (Corkwood)

Corkwood belongs to the Proteaceae family. Only two genera in this big family are represented in Central Australia, *Hakea* and *Grevillea.* Corkwood is a small, gnarled tree, up to 6 m tall, with thick, corky bark, deeply fissured. The long, narrow leaves, up to 30 cm, are circular in cross-

Eremophila longifolia
(Weeping Emu Bush)

Eremophila latrobei
(Latrobe's Desert Fuchsia)

Eremophila longifolia
(Weeping Emu Bush)

Eucalyptus opaca (Bloodwood)

See page 81 for a brief description of the genus *Eucalyptus.*

Bloodwoods have tessel-lated or pavement-like bark. They are usually trees 6 to 11 m tall, sometimes taller. The dull green adult leaves are not opposite and are long and narrow, 10 to 15 cm x 1 to 2 cm. The buds are in clusters of three to

Eucalyptus opaca
(Bloodwood)

Hakea suberea (Corkwood)

Hakea suberea (Corkwood)

Eucalyptus opaca
(Bloodwood)

section. The cream flowers grow in clusters up to 12 cm long. The woody fruit is oval shaped, often swollen in the lower half and with a beaked end. The seed is winged.

137

Rhagodia eremaea
(Ruby Saltbush)

The flower spikes are hemi-spherical and usually 1 to 3 cm long, pale pink and cov-ered with snow-white hairs.

Senna artemisioides ssp. *artemisioides* (Silver Senna)

This silver shrub of the Caesalpiniaceae family is from 1 to 2 m high. The grey to green leaves, 3 to 6 cm long, are divided into leaflets of three to ten pairs. The silvery colour is due to the white, flattened hairs on the leaves. The flowers are sweetly scented, globular cups which grow in a cluster. The rounded petals are 0.7 to 1 cm x 0.5 to 0.7 cm in size. The flat, oblong pod, 4 to 8 cm x 0.6 to 1 cm, is sometimes a shining brown colour.

Ground-storey plants

Ptilotus obovatus (Silvertail)

Silvertails belong to the Amaranthaceae family, commonly known as pussy-tails. The Silvertail is a little shrub 10 to 130 cm tall and across. The flowers are gathered together to form fluffy heads, or 'pussytails'.

Tripogon loliiformis (Five-minute grass)

This grass is a slender annual, rarely over 15 cm

Rhagodia eremaea (Ruby Saltbush)

Rhagodia eremaea (Ruby Saltbush)

R. eremaea belongs to the saltbush or Chenopodiaceae family. It is a rounded shrub up to 2 m high. The leaves are wide and flat, 1 to 2 cm long and have a mealy covering below. The fruit is a red berry about 0.3 cm wide.

Ptilotus obovatus (Silvertail)

Senna artemisioides ssp.
artemisioides (Silver Senna)

Tripogon loliiformis
(Five-minute grass)

Senna artemisioides ssp.
artemisioides (Silver Senna)

high. It forms compact leafy tufts with dense, fibrous butts. The leaf blades are 5 to 7.5 cm long, narrow, flat or loosely folded and finely pointed and mainly occur at the base of the plant. The seed-head is a spike 5 to 8 cm long and up to 0.5 cm wide, erect and pale or olive green. Found throughout the region but particularly on stony tablelands and alluvial areas. The common name of the plant is a reflection of the plant's fast growth after only a little rain.

139

Insects are particularly abundant in the mulga lands' infertile and uncertain environment. Colonies of ants and termites act as storage organs which can buffer the pulses of production brought about by extremes of drought and rain. This dominance by invertebrates anchors the food web which can then ramify into a network of other invertebrate and vertebrate predators. Predictably such an abundance of insects attracts mainly insectivorous birds to mulga woodlands, though nectarivorous birds such as honeyeaters will arrive in numbers during flowering. Large birds such as the Black-faced Cuckoo-shrike will not be found in the mulga woodlands.

Birds

White-browed Treecreeper
Climacteris affinis

This 14 cm desert-dweller is quiet and inconspicuous. It is grey-brown and has a white eyebrow and streaks over the ear. It has bold white stripes on its underparts. A rather solitary and sedentary bird, it hop-gallops methodically up tree trunks and main branches probing for ants and other insects. It is usually silent, making soft cricket-like chirrups but, during breeding, the male chirrups stridently.

Bourke's Parrot
Neophema bourkii

A small, soft-brown parrot with whitish eyering, 19 to 23 cm in length. The pale edgings on the feathers of the wings give a strong pattern. The breast is washed pink, deeper on the abdomen. The male has extensive blue: the forehead-band, bend of the wing, flanks, under the tail and on the sides of the rump are blue. The female is duller. They usually keep to pairs and small parties and gather on the ground to feed. Flight is swift and direct, interspersed with brief glides on partly downswept wings. Contact call in flight is a mellow, repeated 'chu-wee'. It also has a soft, chirrupy twitter. The alarm call is a shrill, metallic note.

Mulga Parrot
Psephotus varius

A slender, bright emerald green parrot with a long tail, 28 cm long including the tail. The male has a scarlet patch on the belly and thighs which is

Mulga Parrot
Psephotus varius

prominent in flight. It has a yellow mark on the forehead and shoulder and a red mark on the back of the head and the rump. The female is duller with a reddish patch on the back of the head and shoulder. They gather in pairs and family parties and forage on the ground for seeds. Their flight is very swift and direct with interrupted wing-beats producing an undulating effect. The contact call is a mellow, flute-like whistle repeated three or four times.

Chiming Wedgebill
Psophodes cristatus

The Chiming Wedgebill is a 19 to 22 cm, brown whip-bird with a brown crest. The middle flight feathers are edged whitish. The tail is prominent and rounded, broadly tipped white. The Chiming Wedgebill is communal with groups of up to 20 occupying a small territory. They feed on the ground and on low branches, picking up insects and seeds with a low dashing flight, fluttering and gliding. They are shy, but their sweetly whistled downward chime of four to six notes is repeated over and over and sounds a little like 'but did you get drunk'.

White-winged Triller
Lalage sueurii

These are migratory birds, up to 18 cm. The male and female have different plumage. The male is glossy black above with a grey rump and pure white below. It has conspicuous white shoulders and white edges to the wing feathers. When the male is not breeding, its black back and crown is replaced with brown. The female is brown above and off-white below, slightly streaked brown and wing-feathers are margined with fawn-white which gives them a distinctive netted pattern. The White-winged Triller nests south of the Tropic of Capricorn in spring and moves north in March–April. Trillers usually travel in groups of 3 to 50. The group forages on beetles, grasshoppers, phasmids and other insects. Flight is swift and graceful with long, loping undulations; and the song, uttered by the male during breeding, is a loud, incessant, musical chatter 'chif-chif-chiff-joey-joey-joey' ending in a canary-like trill.

Little Button-quail
Turnix velox

This highly nomadic little bird, 13 to 15 cm, arrives in numbers when the season is good. It is a small quail with a heavy blue-grey bill and pale eye. The female is tawny to cinnamon above, suffused with grey and whitish below. The male is smaller and has a pattern of darker feather-margins on the sides of his neck and breast. Little Button-quail run like mice and feed on native grass seeds. When flushed they fly low and fast and turn in the air to expose a cinnamon white-edged rump and whitish underparts, before dropping to the ground. Their call is a low 'oom oom' often at night.

Thornbills

Thornbills are the LBBs (little brown birds) of the inland, about 10 cm long. They are endlessly active, usually in parties or small flocks, searching for insects. Look for these features to distinguish them: general colour—grey, brown or greenish-yellow; eye—pale or dark; forehead and crown—plain, scalloped or streaked; breast—plain or streaked; rump—buff, yellow or brown to rusty. Their various calls are distinctive.

Yellow-rumped Thornbill *Acanthiza chrysorrhoa*

The most widespread, largest at 10 to 12 cm and most distinctly marked of the thornbills with a bright yellow rump, white eyebrow, white-spotted black crown and pale eye. It occurs in pairs or small flocks, feeding on the ground, hopping and teetering on its tail. Its bouncing flight exposes a yellow rump which contrasts with the black white-tipped tail. Its voice is a vivacious, merry tinkling with a cyclic pattern.

Chestnut-rumped Thornbill *Acanthiza uropygialis*

A plain thornbill 10 to 11 cm, with a pale chestnut rump, its underparts are whitish and unstreaked and the eye is also whitish. Usually found in small flocks, it feeds on the ground, in

Crimson Chat
Ephthianura tricolor

Yellow-rumped Thornbill
Acanthiza chrysorrhoa

shrubs and low trees. It flies bouncingly, revealing a chestnut rump and contrasting blackish and white-tipped end of the tail. The voice is a penetrating 'see ti ti ti see' and also a pleasant warble based on this sound pattern.

Slate-backed Thornbill *Acanthiza robustirostris*

A smaller, 9.5 cm thornbill. It is the only thornbill with a head and back noticeably blue-grey and a crown with fine, dark streaks. It has a short, robust bill and a red eye. Usually found in pairs, it feeds in foliage. Its voice is a loud 'whippy-chew', single soft 'pseet' and harsh 'thrip thrip'.

Sand Monitor
Varanus gouldii

Southern Whiteface
Aphelocephala leucopsis

The Southern Whiteface is like a thornbill. About 10 to 12 cm, it is grey-brown above with a white mask from above the bill to below the eye, margined black above. It has a broad, black tail band, tipped white. The slightly curved bill is sturdy and the eye is whitish to straw-yellow. It feeds in pairs to small flocks mostly on or near the ground with a continuously teetering tail. The voice is a squeaking 'teeter-teeter' on one note.

Crimson Chat
Ephthianura tricolor

Chats are small (about 10 cm), colourful birds, a bit like honeyeaters but less dependent on nectar. The male has a crimson crown and breast which contrasts with his white throat. He is otherwise brown above except for a crimson rump. The female is brownish with a crimson wash on the rump and breast. Crimson Chats fly in a strong, distinctive, bouncing manner. They travel in groups of tens to hundreds feeding on insects on the ground. The voice is a high-pitched single or multiple 'tseee' and a pleasant warble.

Sand Monitor
Varanus gouldii

Tawny Frogmouth
Podargus strigoides

This 46 cm night bird has a powerful, frog-like beak and fiery-yellow eyes. During the day it camouflages itself by immobilising, compacting its plumage and looking for all the world like a branch. The plumage is bark-grey. Like Kookaburras, the birds snap-up live prey in a swoop from a branch. Large invertebrates and small vertebrates are prey. Their voice is a soft, but penetrating, 'oom-oom-oom'.

Reptiles

A food web anchored in invertebrates will ramify into a network of insect-eating predators. As a result, many lizards inhabit mulga woodlands. All the lizards that are described in the desert ranges and riverine habitats can also be found in the mulga woodlands. Below are others that are commonly seen. Here we introduce the skink genus *Ctenotus*. The following chapter, which describes the sand-dune habitat, has more information about this, the largest group of lizards in Australia (see page 161).

Goannas

(monitor lizards)

Sand Monitor
Varanus gouldii

A widespread and variable species, the colour of the Sand Monitor ranges from yellow to blackish. It is flecked and dotted with lighter and darker colours which often form a banded appearance. The limbs are usually spotted cream. There is usually an obvious black stripe along the temple. The tail is light brown to black with lighter scales tending to form rings. It grows to about 1.6 m. It shelters in burrows, hollow logs or litter and forages on insects, reptiles, birds, mammals and carrion.

Gilbert's Dragon *Lophognathus gilberti*

Dragons

Gilbert's Dragon
Lophognathus gilberti

Gilbert's Dragon is a reddish-brown dragon with two distinctive pale stripes on

Ctenotus leonhardii

either side of the backbone. There is a broad, dark brown bar between the eye and the ear. The upper and lower jaws are white, making the lizard appear to be

Ctenotus schomburgkii

Skinks

See page 161 for a brief description of the genus *Ctenotus*.

Ctenotus leonhardii

There seem to be as many designs on a *Ctenotus* skink as there are Aboriginal dot-painting designs. *Ctenotus leonhardii* is a brown to reddish-brown striped lizard. It has two particularly distinct white strips from the ear to the tail. Its neck and along its side are spotted white. It is about 15 cm long. While this is a widespread lizard, it seems to have a penchant for spiders which are particularly abundant in mulga.

Ctenotus schomburgkii

This skink is usually a rich, coppery-brown, gradually merging with olive-brown colouring on the rump and tail. It has a series of white, black and coppery brown stripes and has a line of coppery dots along its sides. It grows to about 8 cm long.

wearing pale lipstick but which extends to past the ear. A row of spines at the back of the neck extend to a ridge along the lizard's back. This is often a tree-dwelling lizard, with a total length of about 40 cm.

Honey Pot Ant
Camponotus inflatus

Ants

Mulga Ant
Polyrachus macropus

Perhaps more than any other habitat, mulga is dominated by ants. The most conspicuous features of the Mulga Ant are its mounds which are obvious after even a brief walk in a mulga woodland. These mounds are built as a response to transient flooding which, in this habitat, results in water sheeting across the entire landscape.

Honey Pot Ant
Camponotus inflatus

The colonies of these ants

Mulga ant nest

open in a series of small ruptures at the base of mulga trees. A favoured bush food of Aboriginal people, Honey Pot Ants force-feed a certain group of their colony which hang upside down on the ceiling of a vault until their abdomens blow up to form a marble-sized honey pot.

CHAPTER EIGHT

Sand-dunes and Sand-plains

Introduction

The sand-dunes and plains of Central Australia are the home of the spinifex grasslands. Often known as hummock grasslands, this ecosystem, more than any other, characterises the deserts of the inland. The grasses have a characteristic growth form: a clump of regularly and closely branched long stems from which leaf blades stand out at narrow angles. The effect of this regular pattern of growth in all directions is a hemispherical hummock. The root system of each hummock is diffuse and deep and evenly distributed down to at least 3 m. Generally the roots develop from the same nodes as the shoots, so that each stem has its own personal water and nutrient supply—an advantage in such a desiccated environment. Being stiff, the roots seem to prop up the tussock giving it rigidity.

During their first dry period, the flat leaf blades of the grasses become permanently folded. In effect this means that only one side of the leaf is exposed to the drying air, the other side of the leaf being curled in on itself. The leaves are

also sclerophyllous, that is, they are very hard and fibrous and have silicon gran-
ules, called phytoliths, embedded in their epidermis, like microscopic bits of
glass. When the leaves become folded, the steel-sharp tips project outwards and
strongly discourage intending grazers and passing tourists.

Even though there are 30 species, only a few are widespread and they cover
large expanses of arid Australia. 'Soft' Spinifex *(Triodia pungens)* and Feather-top
Spinifex *(Plectrachne schinzii)*, form most of the communities of the sand-plains
and some arise on sand-ridges to the north and west of Alice Springs. 'Hard'
Spinifex *(Triodia basedowii)* is the most drought-resistant species and is common
south of Alice Springs, especially in the Simpson Desert.

Spinifex flourishes in conditions of low rainfall and infertile soils. It also
flourishes under a regime of frequent fire; surviving by committing suicide in a
blaze of glory. High flammability due to its dryness and volatile resin in its cells is
a feature of spinifex. Like other plant formations, spinifex steadily accumulates
biomass after rainfall events but, unlike other plant formations, it does not easily
break down and it maintains most of this flammable material throughout its life-
time. In this way it seems to actually encourage fire so that the subsequent
passage of wildfire is of unparalleled speed and intensity; a holocaust with con-
vection columns producing enormous, black mushroom clouds.

Fire is a major environmental factor in the modern Australian environment and those in spinifex burn perhaps every five years. Not surprisingly, the trees and shrubs that are commonly scattered across spinifex grasslands have evolved various recovery strategies to cope with fire. Some, like *Grevillea* species, *Hakea* species and the Desert Oak *(Allocasuarina decaisneana)* survive fire because they have a thick, corky bark which protects their living tissue. These perennial plants also regrow from unburnt tissue such as epicormic buds (on stems) and ligno-tubers (underground).

Others, such as *Acacia* species and the short-lived forbs, store seed in the soil. Fire enhances seed germination in these species restoring populations of individual plants. Others again, have seeds which blow into a burnt area from outside. The Desert Poplar, *Codonocarpus cotinifolius*, is a common plant growing in spinifex after fire and recolonises by the wind-dispersal of its seeds.

Some species seem to rise from the ashes. These short-lived fireweeds, such as the appropriately named Fire Bush (*Senna pleurocarpa*) flourish after fire. From a satellite view, spinifex grasslands look like so many artist's brush-strokes. The mosaic of subtle yellows and reds represent the different stages of plant recovery after fire. Different plant groups grow at different times depending on the amount and timing of local rainfall.

Topography is another factor which adds to the mosaic-like complexity of the spinifex grasslands. For instance, in the dune fields surrounding Uluru, *Thryptomene maisonneuvei* forms pure stands on dune slopes and dune crests in 'old' fire areas. The shrub is less flammable than spinifex and the clumping affords some protection against fire. On recently burned areas, however, *Calotis erinacea* and *Chrysocephalum semicalvum* grow. Some species occur in almost all spinifex areas, having their highest cover in the early post-fire period. *Leptosema chambersii* and *Scaevola*

Acacia aneura (Mulga)

parvifolia are two which, incidentally, produce abundant nectar and fruit soon after fire. As a general rule, while perennials (such as spinifex) occupy a limited area in this early post-fire period, short-lived grasses and forbs fill the spaces. As perennials dominate, short-lived species disappear and there is a slow but certain dominance by scattered woody perennials and abundant spinifex.

Therefore the plants that you notice on sand-plains and dunes will vary from year-to-year depending on when the last fire passed through and how soon afterwards rain fell.

Turning to the animals of the spinifex grasslands, unlike other grasslands in the world, spinifex does not have a complement of large, herbivorous mammals like the herds of gazelle, wildebeest and zebra found in East Africa. On the contrary, termites are the miniature grazing animals of the spinifex grasslands. And lizards are the hunters; the Australian answer to tigers, lions and cheetahs. Small carnivorous marsupials and (rather large) carnivorous invertebrates also occur in the sand-dunes and sand-plains habitat.

You will almost never see the small carnivorous marsupials and rodents that live in this habitat, unless you are trapping them (and letting them go) for research. Tracks and traces (see chapter 3) are the clues to the wildlife wanderings amongst sand-dunes.

PLANTS OF THE SAND-DUNES AND SAND-PLAINS

Acacia aneura (Mulga)

See page 74 for a brief description of the genus *Acacia*.

Acacia aneura (Mulga)

See also page 131.

Mulga occurs in many different shapes so that it can often be difficult to identify. It mostly occurs on the red earth plains surrounding the ranges and looks like an umbrella blown inside-out. On the plains the tree can grow to 15 m. The much smaller, untidy tree that grows on the rocky slopes of the ranges usually has branches growing straight out and grows in stunted, open stands because of the poor water supply in the rocky substrate. The tree often looks grey with silvery tips. The flowers grow in spikes, 1.5 to 3 cm long. The papery pods are short and flat, 1.5 to 5 cm x 0.4 to 1.5 cm.

Acacia aneura (Mulga)

Acacia dictyophleba
(Waxy Wattle)

Acacia dictyophleba (Waxy Wattle)

This waxy acacia grows as a bushy shrub up to 3 m high. It can be recognised by the white, waxy patches on its phyllodes. These are

Acacia georginae (Gidgee)

Acacia georginae (Gidgee)

narrow and elliptical in shape with dimensions normally 3 to 8.5 cm x 0.4 to 1.5 cm. The veining of the phyllodes can best be seen by holding a leaf against the light. The flower-heads are globular and have 30 to 60 flowers. The pods are straight, flat and narrow and about 9 cm long.

Acacia georginae (Gidgee)

This spreading, often straggly tree grows to 5 m. It is often multi-trunked. The

Acacia georginae (Gidgee)

tree has a dense crown and offers deep shade. The phyllodes are narrow and tapered toward both ends, 4 to 11 cm x 0.4 to 1.6 cm. The globular flower-head has 12 to 25 flowers. The pods are curved, 6 to 13 cm x 1.2 to 2.5 cm. In humid or rainy weather the tree can give off an unpleasant smell, rather like cat's urine.

Acacia kempeana (Witchetty Bush)

Commonly known as Witchetty Bush because Aboriginal people eat witchetty grubs from the roots, *A. kempeana* grows as a spreading shrub or tree up to 5 m tall. The grey-green phyllodes are narrow and elliptical, 3 to 7.5 cm x 0.4 to 1.5 cm and have rounded ends. The flower-heads are golden spikes about 1 to 2 cm long. The papery pods are flat, about 5 cm x 1 cm.

Acacia ligulata
(Umbrella Bush)

Umbrella bush is a spreading bush or tree and grows up to 5 m. The phyllodes are

Acacia kempeana
(Witchetty Bush)

variable, though normally linear, 3 to 10 cm x 0.2 to 2 cm and erect, not drooping, with a blunt, hooked end and often having the appearance of being chewed by bugs. The flowers are golden and globular with 18 to 28 flowers on each flower-head. The pods are long and twisted, 12 cm x 0.5 to 1 cm and constricted

between the seeds. The seeds have a bright red or yellow aril attached to them.

Acacia murrayana
(Colony Wattle)

Colony Wattle, as the name suggests, grows extensively in colonies. Colony Wattle is a shrub or tree growing to 5 m high. The branches have a whitish, waxy covering. The leaves are long, flat and narrow, 5 to 18 cm x 0.2 to 1 cm, with a central vein. The globular

Acacia ligulata
(Umbrella Bush)

Acacia kempeana
(Witchetty Bush)

flower-heads are deep golden and contain 25 to 50 flowers. The heads are in clusters. The light brown, papery pods, 8 cm x 1 cm, are flat and raised over the seeds.

Acacia ramulosa
(Horse Mulga)

Horse Mulga is often hard to distinguish from common Mulga (*Acacia aneura*). Horse Mulga is a bushy shrub or spreading tree up to 5 m high. The pyllodes

151

Allocasuarina decaisneana (Desert Oak)

The Desert Oak belongs to the Casuarinaceae family. It is found in the sand-dune areas west and south of the Alice and usually grows along ancient watercourses or 'fossil rivers'. The Desert Oak is a beautiful, weeping tree, growing to 15 m. It has a stout trunk with thick, deeply fissured bark. Branchlets are pendulous, jointed and striated. The leaves are reduced to scales, four scale-leaves to each joint. There are separate male and female flowers. The flowers have no petals. The fruit is a cone and the seeds have wings.

Acacia murrayana
(Colony Wattle)

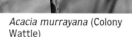

Acacia murrayana (Colony Wattle)

are flat to circular in cross-section, 6 to 20 cm x 0.1 to 0.3 cm, rigid and pointing upward. The phyllodes are finely hairy. The flowers are in spikes, 0.5 to 1.8 cm long. The pods are distinguished from those of Mulga being pendulous and cylindrical, 7 to 13 cm x 0.5 to 0.8 cm and having a hairy covering.

Allocasuarina decaisneana
(Desert Oak)

Acacia ramulosa
(Horse Mulga)

Codonocarpus cotinifolius (Desert Poplar)

The Desert Poplar belongs to the uniquely Australian Gyrostemonaceae family. It is a tree or tall shrub growing to 10 m. The pale green

Acacia ramulosa
(Horse Mulga)

leaves are broad and up to 6 cm long with a pointed or rounded end. The male and female flowers are usually on separate trees and consist of a small, lobed ring (no petals) about 0.5 cm in diameter. The fruits are bell-shaped (*Codonocarpus* means 'bell-shaped fruit'), 1 to 1.5 cm long. The trees are short-lived and grow rapidly after fire.

Codonocarpus cotinifolius
(Desert Poplar)

Eremophila wilsii (Sandhill Native Fuchsia)

Dodonaea viscosa ssp. *angustissima* (Hopbush)

Hopbush belongs to the family Sapindaceae. The Hopbush is a small, rounded shrub up to 2 m high. The shiny green leaves are oblong, 4 to 8 cm x 0.4 to 0.7 cm, with slightly toothed margins. The orange fruit capsule has three to four wings, each about 5 mm wide. The capsule is usually less than 2 cm long.

Eremophila wilsii (Sandhill Native Fuchsia)

See page 80 for a brief description of the genus *Eremophila*.

*Eremophila wilsii (*Sandhill Native Fuchsia*)*

Sandhill Native Fuchsia will always be found growing in deep sand. It is a small bush, growing to 1.5 m. The short, green leaves are narrow to oval-shaped, 1 to 4.5 cm x 0.4 to 2.1 cm. The leaves have no stalks and the margins are serrate. The large flowers, up to 2 cm long, are usually bright

purple, but may be lilac. They always have a dark throat spot and a fringed, white beard under the upper lip. The fruit is oval with a beak, 0.6 to 1.1 cm x 0.2 to 0.6 cm.

Eremophila longifolia (Weeping Emu Bush)

This shrub to small tree, 1 to 6 m high, has weeping branches. The dull green leaves are narrow and up to 15 cm long, normally sparsely haired. One to three brick red, spotted flowers

Eremophila longifolia
(Weeping Emu Bush)

A mallee which is mostly 3 to 6 m high. The bark is smooth and white or grey coloured. The adult leaves are blue-green in colour and are oval, about 6 to 8 cm x 1 to 1.5 cm and joined in pairs, encircling the stem. The buds occur in clusters of three to seven and the flowers are cream. The small gumnuts, about 0.5 to 0.7 cm, are cylindrical, tapering to the base. The valves are at or below the rim.

Eucalyptus gamophylla
(Blue Mallee)

grow out of the leaf axils. There is an obvious knob at the base of the flowers. The fleshy fruit becomes purple when ripe and is a favoured food of Emus.

Eucalyptus gamophylla (Blue Mallee)

See page 81 for a brief description of the genus *Eucalyptus*.

Eucalyptus gamophylla
(Blue Mallee)

Eremophila longifolia
(Weeping Emu Bush)

155

Eucalyptus opaca (Bloodwood)

Grevillea juncifolia
(Desert Grevillea)

Grevillea eriostachya
(Honey Grevillea)

Honey Grevillea is a straggly, spreading bush, growing to 3 m and shoots from the roots after fire. The leaves are long, up to 25 cm, very narrow and grooved underneath. The green-golden flowers are densely clustered on a spike which extends out on spreading branches. The flowers glisten with nectar. The flower stalks are densely hairy. (The name *eriostachya*

Eucalyptus opaca
(Bloodwood)

Bloodwoods have tessellated or pavement-like bark. They are usually trees 6 to 11 m tall, sometimes taller. The dull green adult leaves are not opposite and are long and narrow, 10 to 15 cm

Eucalyptus opaca
(Bloodwood)

x 1 to 2 cm. The buds are in clusters of three to seven, developing into cream flowers. The large, pink-stalked gum-nuts are oval-shaped —almost urn-like—2 to 2.5 cm wide, with the valves inside.

Genus *Grevillea*

Grevilleas belong to the Proteaceae family. In Central Australia the family is represented by hakeas and grevilleas. The flowers of *Grevillea* are on short stalks in cylindrical bottlebrush-like clusters. The leaves are strap-like, narrow or cylindrical. The fruit is a hard (but not thickly wooded as in *Hakea*), round or oval capsule which often has a projection. The capsule contains two round seeds which are usually winged all round.

Grevillea juncifolia
(Desert Grevillea)

Grevillea stenobotrya
(Rattlepod Grevillea)

Grevillea stenobotrya (Rattle-pod Grevillea)

Rattlepod Grevillea grows in bushes or clumps up to 5 m high. The leaves are narrow and long, up to 25 cm and grooved underneath. The flowers are cream and grow in narrow, branching clusters (*stenobotrya* means 'narrow cluster') held erect at the ends of branches. The stalks of the flower clusters are not hairy. The seed case is round, flat, about 1 to 1.5 cm long and beaked. They rattle together when dry.

Grevillea eriostachya
(Honey Grevillea)

means 'woolly spike'). The hairy seed case is elliptical and about 2 cm long.

Grevillea stenobotrya
(Rattlepod Grevillea)

Grevillea juncifolia (Desert Grevillea)

Desert Grevillea is a shrub which grows to 6 m high and resprouts after fire. It has rough, grey bark. The leaves are long, up to 22 cm, narrow and striated. The stalks of the flower cluster are sticky and densely hairy. The large, orange flower clusters have abundant nectar and the flowers are hairy. The seed case is round, flattened and hairy.

Gyrostemon ramulosus
(Camel Poison Bush)

Hakea eyreana
(Fork-leafed Corkwood)

Gyrostemon ramulosus
(Camel Poison Bush)

The Camel Poison Bush belongs to the family Gyrostemonaceae which occurs only in Australia. The bush grows as a shrub to 3 m. It is much-branched (*ramulosus* means 'much-branched'). The dark green leaves are linear and grow up to 60 cm long. The lobed, wheel-like flowers are small, about 0.5 cm long and the male and female flowers grow on separate bushes. The lobed fruit is oval or urn-shaped and about 0.8 cm wide and long. The common name comes from the fact that several explorers' camels, including those of Ernest Giles, died after eating the plant.

Hakea eyreana
(Fork-leafed Corkwood)

Belonging to the Proteaceae family, Fork-leafed Corkwood is a small, gnarled tree which grows to 7 m. It has deeply fissured bark. The wiry leaves, circular in cross-section, are much divided and sharp and end in a fork. The bright yellow flowers are in oval clusters about 10 cm long, growing on spikes at the end of the branches. The seed case is rounded and beaked, 1.8 to 2.6 cm and the seeds are winged.

Plectrachne schinzii
(Feathertop Spinifex)

Feathertop Spinifex grows in dense, resinous tussocks about 30 cm high and up to 90 cm wide. The numerous flowering culms (see Figure 9, page 93) are rigidly erect and 1.2 to 1.5 m high. The stems are smooth and hairless, strongly branched at the lower nodes and often pale purple. The leaf blades grow up to 25 cm long and they are smooth, shiny and needle-like (*Plectrachne* means 'Spear point'). The leaf blades are gummy near the stem and also have scattered drops of resin on the surface. The seed-heads are dense and the flowers or florets are carried within spikelets (see Figure 9). The florets are held cupped in large leaf-like bracts called glumes, 1.5 to 2 cm long and these remain on the plant after the mature florets have fallen giving the plant a glistening silvery or feathertop appearance.

Senna pleurocarpa
(Fire Bush)

A tough, straggly shrub, 1 to 3 m high, which frequently suckers to form colonies. The leaves are 7 to

Plectrachne schinzii
(Feathertop Spinifex)

Triodia basedowii
(Hard Spinifex)

15 cm long, with five to nine pairs of well-spaced leaflets, 2 to 5 cm x 0.6 to 1.2 cm. The leaflets are oblong-shaped and often yellow-green. The chocolate-scented, yellow flowers are clustered along a stem 7 to 15 cm long. The pod is wide and flat, 4 to 5.5 cm x 1 to 1.6 cm, with transverse ridges, like ribs, between the seeds (*pleurocarpa* means 'ribbed pod').

Thryptomene maisonneuvei (Desert Heath Myrtle)

As the common name suggests, Desert Heath Myrtle belongs to the Myrtaceae, or myrtle, family. Desert Heath Myrtle forms pure stands on the slopes and crests of dunes in Uluru National Park. *Thryptomene* means 'made small' and Desert Heath Myrtle is a small, much-branched shrub up to 1.5 m high. The bark peels in thin, red strips. The small, thick, overlapping leaves have no stalks and neither do the

flowers. These are pink or white and have five oval petals, each about 0.2 cm in diameter. The fruit develops inside a woody cup.

Triodia basedowii (Hard Spinifex)

See also page 92

Hard Spinifex forms compact or straggly and irregular tussocks, 22 to 37 cm high and up to 75 cm wide. The flowering stems grow up to 120 cm high. The plants are not resinous. They form rings with open centres, as much as 7.5 m across. The hairless and smooth stems are somewhat bent at the nodes. The flowering stem has one to three nodes and long internodes. The leaves have woolly hairs at the base. The blades are up to 25 cm long, narrow, sharply pointed and needle-like. The seed-head is up to 13 cm long and 2.5 cm wide. It can be loose to dense. This is one of the most common grasses in Central Australia, with a geographical distribution of almost half the area of Central Australia.

Triodia pungens (Soft Spinifex)

See also page 92

Soft Spinifex forms straggly and irregular tussocks, 23 to 90 cm high and 15 to 150 cm wide. It does not normally form rings. The base of the leaf, where it is curled around the

Triodia basedowii
(Hard Spinifex)

stem in a sheath, is gummy. The leaves are relatively slender and needle-like with a sharp, but not hard, point (this is why the plant is euphemistically called 'soft' spinifex). A characteristic of the plant is the production of runners from which new plants develop. Soft Spinifex grows mainly in the north of the region. It only grows in favourable areas in the southern part of the region.

Thryptomene maisonneuvei
(Desert Heath Myrtle)

ANIMALS OF THE SAND-DUNES AND SAND-PLAINS

Birds

Spinifexbird
Eremiornis carteri

Birds need a constant supply of food. Therefore in habitats like the monotonous spinifex sand-sheets where little water exists, nomadic birds arrive in explosive numbers after rain. Examples include Budgerigars, Zebra Finches and Crimson Chats. As conditions deteriorate the nomadic birds move on.

Spinifexbird
Eremiornis carteri

This little, 15 cm warbler occupies a particularly arid habitat and, as its name suggests, prefers mature spinifex. It is a plain brown bird with buff white below. Its crown is a little more rufous. It is not rare but is very localised, sedentary and hides when disturbed. The diet includes insects, beetles, grasshoppers and seeds, the bird hopping over the ground and working the bushes. The Spinifexbird flutters weakly from hummock to hummock, its tail appearing heavy and pumping up and down. Its voice is a warbling 'te tee te too', a grating 'chuk', or short, sharp 'kik'.

Rufous-crowned
Emu-wren
Stipiturus ruficeps

This is the lightest-bodied bird in Australia, weighing 5 grams or less and about 12 cm long including its feathery tail. Its upperparts and wings are rufous-brown, its crown is bright rufous. In the male, the face and throat are a deep blue and in the female they are streaked white. The rest of the underparts are cinnamon. These sedentary birds form loose groups of 10 or 20 in the spinifex plains of Central Australia. They rarely hop onto open ground, preferring the shelter of shrubs and hummocks of spinifex to glean for insects. They chirp to each other constantly. They also have a high-pitched, tinny reel.

Reptiles

If there is one animal that is universally successful in arid areas it is the lizard. This is because it 'costs' less to be cold-blooded and not have to maintain a constant temperature in areas of extreme heat and cold. Lizards can also 'switch-off' during periods of stress and perhaps the most stressful of all environments in Central Australia are the sand-dunes and sand-plains. This is where infertility and aridity reach their peak. It is also where the diversity of lizards reaches its peak. Take a walk through some spinifex country and it won't be long until you see a lizard scurrying away. What you see is only the tip of the monolith. Most of the evidence of activity is written in the sand as tracks and traces (see chapter 3). Below are some of the more common lizards and snakes you may glimpse. Include, as well, all the skinks and geckos from the other habitats.

Central Netted Dragon *Ctenophorus nuchalis*

The most spectacular use of all the dimensions of a habitat occurs in the skink *Ctenotus*. And, not surprisingly, spinifex has been intimately involved with the evolution of this genus. *Ctenotus* are slender and secretive lizards apparently

Skinks: The *Ctenotus* genus

these have evolved longer hind legs to make escape from predators more effective. Others forage within the tussocks. While they all

specialist and is also active at night.

The ecological coexistence of so many similar animals, then, is done by clever manipulation of body size, use of habitat and micro-habitat and clocking on and off at different times. In

Centralian Bluetongue *Tiliqua multifasciata*

adapted to 'swimming' through spinifex and because they flee into spinifex clumps at the slightest disturbance, they are rarely seen by humans. Two goannas in particular, *Varanus eremius* and *Varanus gouldii*, prey on *Ctenotus*, as do the elapid snakes (of the venomous Elapidae family), making them a wary and nervous creature.

Thirty-eight of the 78 species of *Ctenotus* occur in arid Australia. But only in the desert-dwellers do up to 11 species coexist, rather tightly packed ecologically speaking. Some forage between plants in the open space: as a rule

eat large amounts of termites, they are opportunistic feeders taking whatever prey they encounter. Differences in body sizes, mean that large lizards concentrate on large prey and small lizards on small items. Those with higher body temperatures are active in the middle of the day and those with lower body temperatures are active when the temperatures are cooler, some even becoming most active in winter. The Panther Skink (*Ctenotus pantherinus*), an exquisitely patterned lizard with light coloured spots with dark borders, is one of these 'cool' lizards. It is a termite

other words, lizards are so 'well-made' for the spinifex ecosystem that they can virtually be 'packed' into it.

Centralian Bluetongue *Tiliqua multifasciata*

It may come as a surprise to realise that this 40 cm, plump (and tasty) lizard is really a skink—one of the biggest in the world. It is pale grey or grey-brown above, with a series of broad, pale orange-brown cross-bands. It has a broad, wedge-shaped, black streak from the eye to above the ear. The Centralian Bluetongue is a ground-dwelling skink.

Dragons

Central Netted Dragon
Ctenophorus nuchalis

A brown to reddish-brown dragon with a fine, dark chocolate-brown netted

pattern covering its head and body. It is whitish below. Usually there is a distinctive narrow, pale stripe running along the back from the head to the base of the tail. The limbs are variegated or barred with dark brown. Breeding

Painted Dragon
Ctenophorus pictus

males have a bright orange flushed throat. The Central Netted Dragon has a somewhat blunt head. About 15 cm long, this lizard is often seen perched on a log, rock or roadside verge.

Painted Dragon
Ctenophorus pictus

A blue-grey to reddish-brown dragon, usually with a series of black blotches along its spine. Between the blotches are yellowish, dark-edged bars or rows of pale spots. The flanks are spotted or mottled with dark brown and scattered

Military Dragon
Ctenophorus isolepis

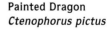

pale, dark-edged spots. Limbs are also mottled. The males are distinctive with grey on the hind part of the throat and black on the forearm. This is a swift-moving lizard about 14 cm long. It prefers low vegetation with dense litter and ground debris such as logs, on which it perches.

Thorny Devil *Moloch horridus*

Thorny Devil
Moloch horridus

You can't mistake this little beauty! It is immediately identifiable by the large, conical spines covering the rather fat and squashed-looking body. It is beaut-ifully patterned with ochre colours. The Thorny Devil is about 15 cm long and feeds exclusively on little black ants.

Thorny Devil
Moloch horridus

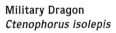

Goannas
(monitor lizards)

Perentie
Varanus giganteus

The Perentie is Australia's largest lizard and second largest in the world after the Komodo Dragon of Indonesia. Growing up to 2 m in length, the Perentie is a rich brown above, its back

Military Dragon
Ctenophorus isolepis

A rich reddish-brown lizard with a pattern ranging from a mixture of dark brown and pale spots, to irregular darker and paler flecks. The Mili-tary Dragon has a pale stripe along its flank and along its side. This swift dragon is about 12 cm long, is closely associated with spinifex and is the most common species seen here.

King Brown Snake
Pseudechis australis

DANGEROUS. A rich copper-coloured to dark olive-brown above, with a cream belly often scattered with dark orange blotches. The individual scales often have darker edges or tips which give the overall impression of a reticulated pattern. The snake is 2 m long, widespread and noc-turnal in the hotter parts of its territory. It feeds on mammals, reptiles and frogs and is found in a wide range of habitats.

and sides sprinkled with creamy-yellow blotches, edged black. On the neck the blotches join to form a distinctive reticulated pat-tern, like paving done with hexagonal-shaped blocks. This ground-dwelling lizard inhabits deep crevices in rocky outcrops but is found also in the adjacent sandy desert. It feeds on carrion and living prey including other lizards.

Sand Monitor *Varanus gouldii*

A widespread and variable species, the colour of the Sand Monitor ranges from yellow to blackish. It is flecked and dotted with lighter and darker colours which often form a banded appearance. The limbs are usually spotted cream. There is usually an obvious black stripe along the tem-ple. The tail is light brown to black with lighter scales tending to form rings. It grows to about 1.6 m. It shelters in burrows, hollow logs or litter and forages on insects, reptiles, birds, mammals and carrion.

Perentie
Varanus giganteus

Sand Monitor
Varanus gouldii

Desert Death Adder
Acanthophis pyrrhus

DANGEROUS. A viper-like snake characterised by a broad, somewhat triangular head, narrow neck, short, stout body and thin, rat-like tail ending in a curved, soft spine. Its colour is reddish-brown. During the day it is found half-buried in sand, soil and litter, usually under a shrub or tree. It attracts prey—mammals and reptiles—by twitching the tip of the tail as a lure.

Desert Death Adder *Acanthophis pyrrhus*

Arthropods

Ants

Spinifex Ant
Ochetellus flavipes

The most obvious feature of this little black ant is the extraordinary runways it builds between spinifex mounds. Apparently it uses these through which to carry certain sun-shy 'bugs' to different spinifex plants. The exudate the bugs produce is harvested by the ants. The ants seem to be 'farming' the bugs.

King Brown Snake *Pseudechis australis*

Melophorus species

This orange ant is a virtual fire-walker and found scudding about when ground temperatures are a scalding 65 degrees Celsius.

Melophorus species

CHAPTER NINE

Chenopod Shrublands and Gibber Plains

Introduction

Toward the southern part of Central Australia, on the way to Uluru (Ayers Rock) or the northern Simpson Desert exists a surreal landscape where creeks bite into ancient limestone plains, making a flat country even flatter. Here, ochre-coloured mesas slowly crumble into gibber plains. In this land of extremes, this is an extreme of another kind; an environment rich in nutrients—even to excess in some elements like calcium, magnesium and sodium—but with no surface water.

The sparseness of the chenopod shrublands growing here, where separate plants can easily be counted, reflects the aridity; but their succulence (a characteristic which is virtually absent from the rest of the sclerophyll-hardened arid zone) hints at its nutritional quality. Today thousands of kangaroos and millions of rabbits confirm it.

Saltbush and bluebush are the main components of the chenopod shrublands: salt-tolerant, desert-loving shrubs. While limestone plains are the home of saltbushes, they are also found on a wide variety of soil types in all positions within the landscape, from skeletal soils of rocky uplands to saline drainage systems.

In the normal extended dry period the ground is bare between the 1 to 3 m high bushes, but after good rainfall it is invisible under a carpet of ephemeral plants.

There is an entirely different suite of invertebrates in the chenopods than in the cellulose-rich spinifex grasslands and mulga woodlands. Termites, for instance, are few and usually found only in the creeklines where there is woody vegetation. Few also are the lizards. Herbivorous grasshoppers, moths and beetles are abundant, as are spiders preying on them and, of course, the ubiquitous ants. Carnivorous marsupials feed on the invertebrates which are often as big as the marsupials, but you will rarely see the secretive marsupials. All, that is, except the Red Kangaroo. Birds, predictably, are not abundant, yet several are restricted to this ecosystem. These include the Gibberbird, the Australian Pratincole and the Inland Dotterel.

Saltbushes

Genera such as *Atriplex*, *Maireana*, *Sclerolaena*, *Chenopodium*, *Enchylaena* and *Rhagodia*, each containing in excess of 30 species, characterise the chenopods.

The following key can assist in determining which of these genera you are looking at:

Plants leafy, the branches not jointed, leaves flat and usually broad, fruiting body is a berry .... *Rhagodia*

Fruiting body dry and the seed enclosed in four to five segments................. *Chenopodium*

Fruiting body dry and the seed enclosed in a hard or spongy body consisting of two small bracts .... *Atriplex*

Leaves narrow, silky-hairy or hairless, fruiting body is a berry without appendages .... *Enchylaena*

Fruiting body with appendages as spines .... *Sclerolaena*

Fruiting body with appendages as a horizontal wing.. *Maireana*

Atriplex sp.

In terms of distribution, the saltbush genus *Atriplex* is one of the most important genera in the arid zone because it forms dominant perennial shrublands and has annual and perennial members which grow in a wide range of communities. Despite this, *Atriplex* is difficult to identify. The common Bladder Saltbush, *Atriplex* *vesicaria*, for instance, has many geographic and edaphic (related to soil type) variants. It seems to be a very 'plastic' species, even changing shape quite considerably under different levels of grazing.

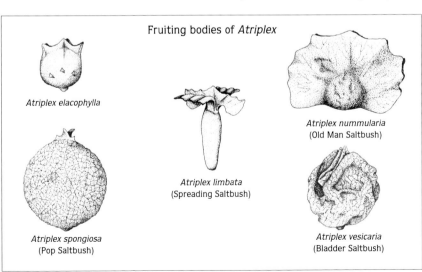

Fruiting bodies of *Atriplex*

Atriplex elacophylla

Atriplex nummularia
(Old Man Saltbush)

Atriplex limbata
(Spreading Saltbush)

Atriplex spongiosa
(Pop Saltbush)

Atriplex vesicaria
(Bladder Saltbush)

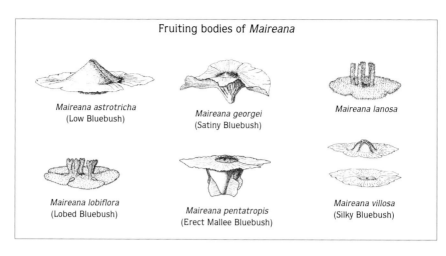

Fruiting bodies of *Maireana*

Maireana astrotricha
(Low Bluebush)

Maireana georgei
(Satiny Bluebush)

Maireana lanosa

Maireana lobiflora
(Lobed Bluebush)

Maireana pentatropis
(Erect Mallee Bluebush)

Maireana villosa
(Silky Bluebush)

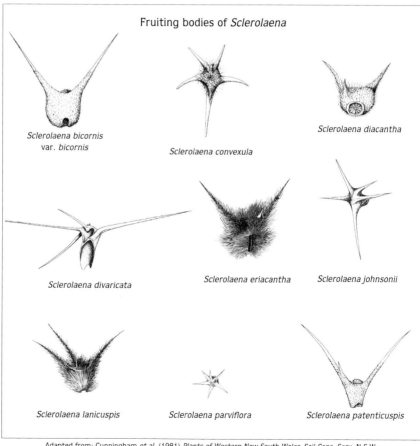

Fruiting bodies of *Sclerolaena*

Sclerolaena bicornis
var. bicornis

Sclerolaena convexula

Sclerolaena diacantha

Sclerolaena divaricata

Sclerolaena eriacantha

Sclerolaena johnsonii

Sclerolaena lanicuspis

Sclerolaena parviflora

Sclerolaena patenticuspis

Adapted from: Cunningham *et al.* (1981) *Plants of Western New South Wales.* Soil Cons. Serv. N.S.W.

ANIMALS OF THE CHENOPOD SHRUBLANDS AND GIBBER PLAINS

Birds

Orange Chat
Ephthianura aurifrons

The male of this small, colourful bird, about 10 to 12 cm, has a yellow body washed orange on its head and breast. The face and throat are black and the rump is yellow. The female has no black on its face and is pale yellowish-grey with a yellow rump and plain yellow-fawn below. Orange Chats forage on the ground in small flocks where they run along quickly, feeding exclusively on insects. They fly in low undulations and are nomadic. They voice a 'check, check', 'cheel-cheel' in flight.

Orange Chat
Ephthianura aurifrons

Gibberbird
Ashbyia lovensis

The Gibberbird is Australia's most complete desert bird. It is a rarely seen chat, about 12 cm, that inhabits the most irradiated gibber plains centred on Lake Eyre, but extending up into the south-east part

of the Northern Territory— if you take the trip down to Andando, you may see them on any of the gibber plains. The Gibberbird is a yellow-breasted chat with a rump the same colour as the back (cinnamon-brown). It has a long-legged upright carriage and charges about on the ground, in groups up to 10, searching for insects. It holds its tail down. They voice a 'wheat-wheat-wheat', 'chip-chip' in flight.

Australian Pratincole
Stiltia isabella

The Australian Pratincole is long-legged, cinnamon brown, with a deep rufous belly patch, short, square tail and long, black wingtips extending beyond the tail, about 23 cm. It has a bi-coloured bill. In flight this bird looks a little like a tern. A migratory bird, it flies north from February to April, returning to the gibber and saltbush plains to breed in September and October. They live in small, loose groups of up to 20 and feed on insects. The voice is a plaintive 'quirra-peet'.

Inland Dotterel
Peltohyas australis

This is one of the most perfectly camouflaged ground birds, almost

Australian Pratincole
Stiltia isabella

impossible to see on the open, sparsely scrubbed gibber plains. It is a medium-sized, 20 cm, sandy coloured plover with a narrow, black, Y-shaped band on the breast and vertical black line through the eye. The under tail-coverts are conspicuously white. During the day a loose group will stand about in the shade of shrubs and eat the leaves of chenopods. At night they disperse and feed on insects. The voice is a metallic 'quoik, krrroot'.

Banded Lapwing
Vanellus tricolor

The Banded Lapwing is a large resident plover with small, red facial wattle, yellow bill and facial skin and a

Inland Dotterel
Peltohyas australis

Bush Thick-knee
Burhinus magnirostris

white bar behind the eye.
The black sides of the neck
continue down to form a
band across the chest. In
flight the white bar across
the wing gives a zigzag
appearance. Banded Lap-
wings live in groups of 5 to
12 and feed on the ground
on invertebrates, seeds and
green plant matter. They
are locally nomadic, following the rain. The voice is a
sad 'er-chill-char...'.

Bush Thick-knee
Burhinus magnirostris

Eerie, wailing calls at night
are usually the only sign
that Bush Thick-knees are
about. It is a long-legged
bird, about 55 cm, grey-
brown above, buff-white
below with a streaked
neck. It moves slowly and
deliberately with the head
often held horizontally.
The bird will freeze when
disturbed, prostrating
itself. It feeds on insects.

Reptiles

Lizards do occur in the
chenopod shrublands, but
nowhere near as abun-
dantly as in the spinifex
grasslands where they
flourish within a food web
based on termite-tidbits.
Particularly common in the
chenopod habitat are
geckos. Dragons such as
the Central Bearded
Dragon, as well as the
widespread goannas—the
Perentie and the Sand
Goanna—are also found.

Geckos

Marbled Velvet Gecko
Oedura marmorata

Soft-bodied nocturnal
lizards, geckos use their
fleshy tongues to keep their
lidless eyes clean. The Marbled Velvet Gecko is a
variable gecko but is typically a yellow-banded,
purplish-brown lizard. It is
about 14 cm long and more-
or-less confined to stony
areas in Central Australia.

Sand Monitor
Varanus gouldii

Tree Dtella
Gehyra variegata

This is a highly variable
gecko, about 12 cm long.
It is grey or purplish-grey
above with irregular blackish marbling. A tree-
dwelling lizard, during the
day it will hide under loose
bark.

Marbled Velvet Gecko
Oedura marmorata

Goannas
(monitor lizards)

Perentie
Varanus giganteus

The Perentie is Australia's largest lizard and second largest in the world after the Komodo Dragon of Indonesia. Growing up to 2 m in length, the Perentie is a rich brown above, its back and sides sprinkled with creamy-yellow blotches, edged black. On the neck

Tree Dtella
Gehyra variegata

the blotches join to form a distinctive reticulated pattern, like paving done with hexagonal-shaped blocks. This ground-dwelling lizard inhabits deep crevices in rocky outcrops but is found also in the adjacent sandy desert. It feeds on carrion and living prey including other lizards.

Sand Monitor
Varanus gouldii

A widespread and variable species, the colour of the

Perentie
Varanus giganteus

Sand Monitor ranges from yellow to blackish. It is flecked and dotted with lighter and darker colours which often form a banded appearance. The limbs are usually spotted cream. There is usually an obvious black stripe along the temple. The tail is light brown to black with lighter scales tending to form rings. It grows to about

1.6 m. It shelters in burrows, hollow logs or litter and forages on insects, reptiles, birds, mammals and carrion.

Dragons

Central Bearded Dragon
Pogona vitticeps

A relatively large, robust lizard, characterised by its broad triangular head and variable-sized body scales. It has a flat body and relatively short tail and an orderly row of spines along the sides of the body. The Central Bearded Dragon is variably coloured from pale grey, to reddish-brown to almost black above. On either side of the spine there is often a series of pale oblong patches. The throat is whitish and the lining of the mouth (which it will display if you get too close) is bright yellow. The throat has a well-developed pouch or beard sporting a border of long, spiny scales.

171

Central Bearded Dragon, *Pogona vitticeps*

Mammals

Marsupials

Red Kangaroo
Macropus rufus

This handsome animal is one of the largest living marsupials in the world. It likes open plains but requires some shade from trees and is seldom found where there are no trees at all. It has a preference for green herbage and its local distribution is influenced by the availability of this. Most males are pale red to brick-red in colour but blue-grey males do exist. Females are usually blue-grey as their common name 'blue-flier' indicates. The male is about 2 m from nose tip to tip of tale and weighs up to 70 kg with the female being smaller and slighter, weighing up to 30 kg.

Red Kangaroo, *Macropus rufus*

GARY STEER

172

CHAPTER TEN

Central Australian Weeds

The remoteness of Central Australia has not protected it from the encroachment of noxious, unwanted and introduced plants. Below is a selection of the weeds likely to be seen in Central Australia. You can aid the conservation of our singular outback environment in a very direct way by reporting occurrences of any of these plants to:

The Department of Primary Industry and Fisheries
PO Box 8760
Alice Springs NT 0871

We thank you for your help.

Mexican Poppy
(Argemone ochroleuca)

A native of Mexico, Mexican Poppy is a bluish-green plant which grows up to 1 m high. It can be found along river systems, moist flats and sand-dunes. The leaves grow up to 20 cm long and are silvery-green with white veining and deep, regular lobes. The upper surface of the leaf is smooth while the underside has a few prickles along the midribs. The leaves are stalkless and clasp onto the cylindrical stem. The stems exude a yellowish, milky sap. Prior to flowering the plant resembles a thistle because of its toothed and prickly leaf margins. The typical Poppy flowers are about 6 cm across, with four light yellow or cream petals. The fruit is a prickly capsule with three to six openings at the top. The capsule contains up to 400 seeds. Mexican Poppy is poisonous to stock but, because it is unpalatable, is rarely eaten.

Mexican Poppy
(*Argemone ochroleuca*)

Noogoora Burr
(Xanthium occidentale)

The Noogoora Burr is a sparingly branched annual plant growing up to 2 m high. The stems and leaves have a rough texture, the leaves are dark green, alternate, 10 to 15 cm in diameter, with three to five irregularly toothed lobes. Female flowers growing in the leaf axils produce clusters of burrs, each 1.5 to 2 cm x 0.5 to 0.8 cm, on short stalks. Hooked spines cover the burr and there are two slightly longer spikes at the end. Noogoora Burr is a native of the Americas and was introduced to Queensland late last century in imported cotton seed. It is toxic if grazed by livestock.

Noogoora Burr
(*Xanthium occidentale*)

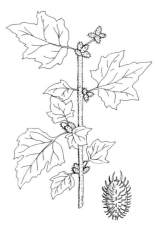

Bathurst Burr
(*Xanthium spinosum*)

Bathurst Burr
(*Xanthium spinosum*)

Related to the Noogoora Burr, Bathurst Burr can be distinguished by its smaller, more branched growth habit and narrower, tapering leaves.

Mossman River Grass
(*Cenchrus echinatus*)

An erect grass growing to a height of 30 to 50 cm. The leaves taper towards the

Mossman River Grass
(*Cenchrus echinatus*)

tip. The plant has a number of seed-heads carrying a cluster of spiny burrs, 0.5 mm. The burrs stick to hair and clothing. Originating in tropical America it is widespread and in the Centre found around Alice Springs—in gardens, school yards and around station homesteads. Without the seed-heads, the plant is difficult to distinguish from other grasses.

Prickly Pear
(*Opuntia* spp.)

Prickly Pear is the common term for many large, similar-looking cactus species with succulent stems. Some of the plants grow up to 7 m high and form impenetrable thickets. The fleshy stem or pad is flat and capable of producing its own roots if broken off. The plant is covered with stout, yellow spines. The flowers are yellow to bright orange and grow on the edge of the stem sections. The fruit is red to purple, pear-shaped, fleshy and contains many small hard-coated seeds. Prickly Pears were introduced to Australia in the early days of European settlement, possibly as ornamental shrubs, hedge plants, fodder crops or as a plant host for cochineal insects which were a source of valuable carmine dye.

Saffron Thistle
(*Carthamus lanatus*)

An erect annual plant that grows up to 1 m high. Saffron Thistle has stiff leaves which form a rosette at the base and then alternate along the stem. The leaves

Saffron Thistle
(*Carthamus lanatus*)

are narrow, triangular, 3 to 8 cm long and folded in a distinct downward curve. The leaves are rigidly spined and end in a sharp, strong point. The flowers are yellow, made of numerous florets and form at the end of branches where they are half hidden by large bracts. The grey-brown

Prickly Pear
(*Opuntia* spp.)

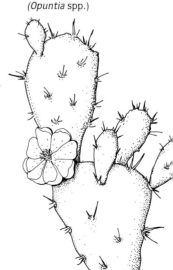

seeds, 0.5 to 0.8 cm long have four prominent ribs and are surrounded by stiff bristles about 0.5 cm long. The seed is heavy, dropping to the base of the plant. Saffron Thistle is a native of the Mediterranean region and probably intro-duced to the Centre in hay and stock feeds from South Australia. Major infesta-tions occur at Kulgera and Erldunda.

Khaki Weed
(Alternanthera pungens)

Khaki Weed forms thick mats on the ground. Leaves, 1 to 3 cm long, are rounded with a slight taper. Flowers are yellow to green and found in dense clusters

Khaki Weed
(Alternanthera pungens)

in the axils of the leaves. Each flower is surrounded by stiff, pointed bracts. The plant dries off in summer after producing large quan-tities of seed which stick to shoes, tyres and swags. Khaki Weed is a native of tropical America.

Caster Oil Plant
(Ricinus communis)

A tall, branching shrub with stout, hollow stems, reaching a height of 2 to 3 m. The leaves are arranged alternately along the branches and are 30 cm or more in diameter. The leaves are divided into seven to nine roughly tri-angular, toothed lobes, each with a central vein radiating from the top of the leaf stalk. Young leaves are glossy, dark reddish-brown, becoming glossy green when mature. They have a distinctive, unpleas-ant odour when crushed. The flowers have no petals and are crowded in stout, erect spikes in the forks of the upper branches. Female flowers occur at the top of the spikes and male flowers at the bottom. The three-lobed fruits, 2.5 cm long, are covered in red or green soft spines. Each lobe con-tains a large, smooth, greyish seed, resembling an engorged cattle tick. When ripe, the fruits explode, throwing the seeds a dis-tance of several metres. A native of Asia and Africa, it is found in Central Australia along the Finke River and in dumps and degraded areas. The seeds, which yield castor oil, are extremely poison-ous and the consump-tion of two to eight seeds by humans can be lethal.

Rubber Bush
(Calotropis procera)

Rubber Bush is a deep-rooted perennial shrub growing to 2.4 m high. Opposite, oval-shaped, fleshy, green-grey

Caster Oil Plant
(Ricinus communis)

leaves, are 10 to 20 cm x 10 cm, with no leaf stalk. Stems and leaves exude a milky, white sap if cut or broken. The bark is whitish and deeply fissured. Clus-ters of attractive, five-petalled, white flowers with purple tips and a central purple crown develop on stalks at the end of branches. The fruit is oval-

Rubber Bush
(Calotropis procera)

175

Athel Pine
(*Tamarix aphylla*)

shaped, grey-green, 7.5 to
10 cm long, and bursts
open to release large quan-
tities of flat, brown seeds,
each with a parachute of
silky hairs.

Athel Pine
(Tamarix aphylla)

A spreading tree, to 10 m
high, with spreading,
jointed branches. Since this
is a flowering plant, it is not
a true pine or conifer. The
trunks have thick, rough,
dark grey to black bark and
the stems are grey-brown.
The trees have a strong,

Paterson's Curse
(*Echium plantagineum*)

woody rootstock with an
extensive web of deeply
penetrating roots. The tiny
leaves are dull, grey-green
and form a sheath around
the fine branchlets, giving
them the appearance of
pine-needles. The flowers
are pinkish-white and small,
growing as spikes 3 to 4 cm
long at the ends of the pre-
vious year's branches. The
fruit is bell-shaped. The
numerous seeds are tiny
and wind-transported but
as they are viable for only a
few weeks, vegetative
reproduction from broken
branches carried by flood
waters is more common. A
native of northern Africa,
the Arabian Peninsula, Iran
and India, it was introduced
to Australia in 1930 where
it was planted as a shade
tree. It has now invaded
the Finke River, the largest
river system in Central Australia.

Paterson's Curse
(Echium plantagineum)

Also called Salvation Jane,
this plant is an erect,
coarsely hairy, winter- and
spring-growing annual.
Autumn seedlings are
large, flat, dark green
rosettes up to 30 cm across
with broad, oval-shaped
leaves. In spring, erect
flowering stems with short

bristles and lance-shaped
leaves, 3 to 9 cm long
appear. The bluish-purple
tubular flowers, said to
resemble Salvation Army
bonnets, are 2 to 3 cm long
and align themselves on
one side of the flowering
spike. A native of the Mediterranean, it has spread
along the South Australian
and Northern Territory border and in Alice Springs
along roadsides where
seeds have been introduced
by vehicles from the southern states.

Goats Head *(Acanthos-*
permum hispidum)

Goats Head is an erect,
annual plant that grows 30
to 80 cm high. It has lobed,
opposite leaves 6 cm x 3
cm. The stems, which fork
repeatedly, are covered
with rough hairs. Groups of
four to six burrs radiate
from central points on the
stems. These burrs are triangular in shape and are
covered with short spines.
Two longer spines give the
appearance of a goat's
head. A native of South
America, it is widely distributed in the Centre.

Goats Head
(*Acanthospermum hispidum*)

References

Anderson, A. (1991). *The Ants of Southern Australia, A Guide to the Bassian Fauna*. CSIRO Australia.

Buckley, R. (1981). 'Soils and vegetation of the central Australian sandridges III. Sandridge vegetation of the Simpson Desert'. *Australian Journal of Ecology* 6, 405-22.

Cogger, H. G. (1992). *Reptiles and Amphibians of Australia*. Reed Books, Sydney.

Jessop, J. (ed.) (1981). *Flora of Central Australia*. Reed Books. Sydney.

Lazarides, M. (1970). *The Grasses of Central Australia*. Australian National University Press. Canberra.

Perry, R.A. (1962). *General Report on Lands of the Alice Springs Area, Northern Territory, 1956-57*. CSIRO Land Research Series No 6. Melbourne.

Pizzey, G. (1980). *A Field Guide to the Birds of Australia*. Angus and Robertson. Sydney.

Schodde, R. and Tidemann, S. (1986). *Readers Digest complete book of Australian birds*. Readers Digest Services, NSW.

Slater, Peter, Slater, Pat and Slater, Raoul. (1986). *The Slater Field Guide to Australian Birds*. Rigby. Sydney.

Strahan, R. (1983). *The Australian Museum Complete Book of Australian Mammals*. Angus and Robertson.

Thomson, B. (1991). *A Field Guide to Bats of the Northern Territory*. Conservation Commission of the Northern Territory. Government Printer. Darwin.

Urban, A. (1990) *Wildflowers and Plants of Central Australia*. Southbank Communications Group. Melbourne.

van Oosterzee, P. (1991). *The Centre—the natural history of Australia's desert regions*. Reed Books. Sydney.

Acknowledgments

Many people have spent hours of their hard-won time assisting with the compilation of this book. First and foremost were the scientists, planners and administrators (hope that covers everybody) of the Conservation Commission of the Northern Territory, and its Director Matti Urvett, without whose help this book would not have come about. In particular, Penny would like to thank Grant Allan who responded to her demands with grace and professionalism. Peter Brocklehurst, Greg Leach and Michael Barritt worked overtime for her and Greg Leach and David Albrecht were always available on the other end of the phone or fax and David, in addition, went out of his way to point Reg to the right plants. Murray Fuller (Department of Primary Industries and Fisheries) provided the information for us to write an important section on the weeds of Central Australia. Noel Preece (Ecoz—Ecology Australia) provided data for the mulga woodlands, helped guide the reptile and mammal selection and helped identify species from unlabelled slides. John Read (Western Mining Corporation, Roxby Downs) helped with the data for the chenopod shrublands, an ecosystem that requires much more research on its wildlife. Alan Anderson (CSIRO), that crusader of ant's rights, helped with, you guessed it, ants! We would also like to thank Michael Barritt, Bill Binns, Ralph Buckley (Griffith University), Russell Grant, Tony Forde, Dal Hartley, Chris Jameson (Department of Mines and Energy), Ian King, Carmel Leonard, Delia Russell, Bill Ryan, Bruce Thomson (Queensland National Parks and Wildlife Service), Stuart Traynor, Rob Worrall, Owen Price and John Zabo. Ken Johnson, Mike Flemming, Dave Gibson, Don Langford and Peter Latz helped review drafts. We would like to thank Bill Templeman and Mary Halbmeyer of Reed Books with whom it has been a pleasure to work. The base art for the maps in Part 1 was done by Alan Puckett and the bird illustrations in Part 2 by Peter Slater. For generously providing pictures of species otherwise unavailable to us, we are especially grateful to Hal Cogger. Leoni Cohen patiently helped with the index.

Information was drawn extensively from other books and these need to be mentioned here. For the plants, we have drawn extensively on two books *Flora of Central Australia*, ed. J. Jessop and *Wildflowers* and *Plants of Central Australia* by Anne Urban whose practical, handy field guide took much of the pain out of deciphering complicated technical terms. For the grasses, we also used *The Grasses of Central Australia* by M. Lazarides. For the birds we used information from three books: Graham Pizzey's *A Field Guide to the Birds of Australia*; *The Slater Field Guide To Australian Birds*; and the *Readers Digest Complete Book of Australian Birds* by R. Schodde and S. Tidemann. For the mammals we drew on Ronald Strahan's *The Australian Museum Complete Book of Australian Mammals*. For the reptiles, who can go past Hal Cogger's masterpiece *Reptiles and Amphibians of Australia*. The detailed references are given for these in the references and we commend them to all readers who want more detailed knowledge on the various aspects of Central Australia's most amazing natural history.

The Northern Territory Department of Mines and Energy generously allowed us to use information contained in their excellent pamphlets: Macdonnell Ranges Guide, Geology and Landforms, Alice Springs to Glen Helen; Macdonnell Ranges Guide, Geology and Landforms, Alice Springs to Arltunga; and Astro-geological Features of Central Australia.

Finally Penny would like to thank, once again, her beloved husband and partner in life Noel Preece (who also edited part of the book) totally delightful son Luke Preece and mother Henny van Oosterzee, whose loving support is of inestimable value. Without them what would be the purpose.

Index